How a Champion Is Made

Blueprints Series

By
STEVE CARDILLO

with
Marc Zappulla

D0967994

Disclaimer

The focus of this publication is to offer insightful material on the content outlined. The publisher and the author make no claims or assurances with regard to the accuracy or wholeness of the subject matter of this work and explicitly deny all warranties, including, without limitation, warranties of fitness or nutrition for an exacting purpose. The recommendations and policies contained herein may not be suitable for every instance.

Furthermore, the publisher and author are not committed to rendering physical or mental health, or any other example of personal or professional services depicted in this book. The reader should consult with his or her primary medical, or mental health physician, or any other competent professional before implementing any of the proposals or ideals in this book or drawing conclusions from it. The publisher and author deny all responsibility for any liability, injury, physical or mental, loss or risk, personal or otherwise, which may have been sustained as a consequence, directly or indirectly, of the use or appliance of any of the subject matter in this book. This publication is sold with the conception that the publisher is not engaged in providing legal, accounting, or other professional services. If such assistance is required, the services of a competent professional should be obtained.

None of the original images in this book and cover have been altered, giving exception only in cases where the identity of a minor is protected, or cropping to enhance formatting.

Everett Public Schools
Administration Building

Frederick F. Foresteire
SUPERINTENDENT

Thomas J. Stella, EdD
ASSISTANT SUPERINTENDENT

Charles F. Obremski
ASSISTANT SUPERINTENDENT
OF BUSINESS AFFAIRS

Janice M. Gauthier
DIRECTOR OF CURRICULUM

October 20, 2010

To Whom It May Concern:

Mr. Cardillo worked for six years as a Physical Education teacher in the Everett Public Schools.

During his tenure, parents frequently asked for their children to be placed in his class because of his knowledge and how he conducted his classes. The parents felt their children learned the importance of good health, healthy habits and conditioning programs.

From a personal point, Steve worked with my son when he was a teenager and developed him to the level where, at eighteen years old, he was bench pressing over four hundred pounds and competing in regional competitions.

Most importantly, Steve installed in my son the importance of living a clean life without drugs, alcohol or tobacco. To this day, my son still has never used drugs, alcohol or tobacco and continues to live by the philosophy instilled in him by Mr. Cardillo.

Mr. Cardillo has influenced hundreds of young people in a positive way.

Sincerely yours,

Frederick F. Foresteire
Superintendent of Schools

FFF:gg

121 Vine Street, Everett, Massachusetts 02149   617 389-7950   Fax 617 394-2408

Dear Readers:

I thought I'd share a few thoughts about Steve Cardillo. Steve has been a trusted friend and colleague of mine for over 20 years. Of all of the people I have encountered in my personal and professional life, Steve stands apart as an individual of incredible integrity, honesty, and professional competence.

Currently I am the Chief Marketing Officer for Hasbro, Inc., a company that provides children and families around the world with a wide range of immersive entertainment offerings including toys and games, television programming, motion pictures, and video games (http://www.hasbro.com). I am a graduate of Yale University and Harvard Law School.

I first met Steve when I was working at Reebok International as a licensing and sports marketing executive several years ago. We chose Steve and his company from amongst many to be our partner as we entered the fitness training/equipment category. Steve and Cardillo Inc. were very well known for making the best weight lifting belts in the country, perhaps in the world, which were being used by many professional athletes across a multitude of sports. In addition, Steve was highly respected as a fitness consultant and strength coach/personal trainer, as well as an expert in the field of physical fitness and nutrition. We worked with Steve to incorporate Reebok's THE PUMP technology into a full line of weight lifting belts. Steve also designed, manufactured and marketed Reebok weight lifting gloves.

In addition to being a Reebok marketing partner and licensee, Steve also became a very influential voice in the Reebok C.O.R.P.S. (Circuit of Reebok Professionals and Specialists), which was an elite organization consisting of the world's foremost fitness professionals, including experts on strength and conditioning, personal training, and sports medicine. C.O.R.P.S. members were recognized as the leading and most respected fitness educators, instructors, and consultants; were selected for membership based on their exemplary contributions to the fitness industry; and were instrumental in working in partnership with Reebok to develop leading edge fitness programs that Reebok distributed throughout the world. Steve emerged as a leading member of this organization due to professional and personal credibility, integrity, and credentials.

As a father of four young athletes (3 currently playing varsity high school sports), I am keenly aware of the variety of issues confronting both parents and their children as they train and compete in sports at all levels. Over the years, I have relied upon Steve for advice and counsel on many issues surrounding youth sports and conditioning, including training, nutrition, and injury prevention and recovery. Several years ago I asked Steve to help my son (a football, hockey, and lacrosse player) and daughters (field hockey, ice hockey, lacrosse players) train for their sports. Steve designed customized training and nutritional programs that enabled my children to achieve their full potential, and prepare them for high school and college sports. Steve has consistently demonstrated to me an expansive knowledge of training, conditioning, and nutrition, as well as an uncompromising dedication to providing these children with the very best advice and counsel for their individual needs. Steve has a complete and up-to-date understanding of teenage athletes and what is most effective in helping them achieve their goals.

Foremost among the words I would choose to describe Steve are honest, knowledgeable, generous, and admired. Steve is very well known in the fitness and training community and is respected and admired by his colleagues and competitors alike. Professional athletes have a deep admiration and respect for Steve and the work he has done. Finally, Steve takes his responsibility very seriously and is highly conscientious and trustworthy.

Sincerely,

John Frascotti
Chief Marketing Officer
Hasbro, Inc.
1011 Newport Avenue
Pawtucket, RI

The C.O.R.P.S.

Reebok

FITNESS DIRECTORY
SM

Introduction

Reebok is dedicated to making significant contributions to the fitness industry through the development of quality fitness products, programming, and services. As part of this ongoing commitment, we developed The Circuit of Reebok Professionals and Specialists, (C.O.R.P.S.), an elite organization of fitness professionals and athletes which includes authorities on strength and conditioning, aerobics, Step Reebok^{SM} personal training, and sports medicine.

C.O.R.P.S. members are recognized as the nation's leading and most respected fitness educators, instructors and consultants, and were selected for membership based on their exemplary contributions to the fitness industry. Their credentials, expertise, various services and resources have been compiled for this manual, The C.O.R.P.S. Fitness Directory.

The purpose of The C.O.R.P.S. Fitness Directory is twofold: to serve as a reference guide which offers networking opportunities to health and fitness leaders; and to provide fitness professionals with access to information on professional development and education. In addition to providing information on C.O.R.P.S. members, we have included a listing of Reebok fitness services and an overview of selected industry associations for your reference.

We hope that this directory serves as a valuable resource, and assists you in reaching your professional fitness goals.

9000454

Steve Cardillo, Everett, Massachusetts
Designer, marketing manager, fitness consultant

Personal Profile: Steve, a former National Drug-Free Powerlifting Champion and world record holder, is a professional strength coach and personal trainer. He is currently writing a book on teenage weight training, in which he specializes. Steve has written articles for bodybuilding and fitness magazines and is collaborating with Reebok on the design of fitness products using THE PUMP™ technology. Available for personal training and nutrition consulting.

▼ Personal Training
▼ Corporate Fitness
▼ Business
▼ Coaching (Pro)
▼ Circuit Training
▼ Coaching (H.S.)

To contact any C.O.R.P.S. Member call toll-free: 1-800-435-7022.

Table of Contents

Foreword

When Steve asked me to write a few words about this book, I felt honored and delighted, and did so without hesitation because I believe weight training and nutrition are so interesting. Steve and I have known each other for some time, and as a fitness and sport enthusiast and practicing physician, I greatly admire Steve's motivation and discipline to excel and achieve his goals. During his professional career, he has acquired a great deal of understanding about what it takes to succeed in weight training: motivation, hard work, and knowledge.

While researching and assessing the current publications on weight training, Steve discovered very few that were geared toward young athletes. Personally, I agree with him. I, too, have encountered very few books on weight training targeted specifically for teens. Thus feeling compelled to pass on his knowledge, Steve put pen to paper. Steve's goal is to share with young people the secrets to successful weight training and nutrition. He's the perfect guy to do it.

In this book, Steve conveys the fundamentals which have helped him achieve success for many years. He also shares practical experiences and tips he's learned from working with some of the best professional and nonprofessional athletes from a number of sports disciplines. After reading this book, readers will appreciate that achieving general fitness and success in weight training is never beyond the reach of any young person. If only he and his parents understand what it takes, the sky's the limit.

Indeed, this is what this book is about—one man's personal experiences, struggles, and successes in achieving fitness in general, and weight training in particular throughout his life. Steve takes the readers through a journey of his childhood and adolescence, and along the way, he shares the magic ingredients that have helped him achieve his goals—and I am glad to share with you that these ingredients are all natural, intrinsic or otherwise.

A combination of right nutrition, proper types of exercise, healthy living, as well as a large dose of realistically set goals, motivation, and discipline are the right formula for success. This is what I frequently recommend to most of my patients as well. At first it may sound simple—and yes, it *is* indeed simple—but it is difficult to achieve without proper techniques. How many times do we agree that eating fewer calories and exercising frequently is the necessary prescription for healthful living? And yet, not many of us follow through.

So how can a youngster achieve general fitness and develop a good physique, sense of well-being, confidence, and a healthy self-image from weight training?

This book is invaluable in guiding the young athlete through his quest to achieve all of this and more. Steve brings his own unique perspective on weight training through friendly, conversational instruction. Also, parents and teachers will find that this book dispels many of the myths and lore about weight training for young people.

As a practicing physician and teacher of medicine, I am impressed by Steve's useful tips, helpful instruction, and proper techniques about weight training. And on an inspirational level, Steve reaffirms that hard work, motivation, and discipline are still the necessary ingredients for achieving set goals and ultimately, personal gratification.

—Khiem T. Tran, MD, MHA, FACP
Internal Medicine Attending
Site Residency Program Director
Clinical Assistant Professor of Medicine
University of Illinois, Urbana Champaign, School of Medicine

About the Author

Steve Cardillo

I grew up in the urban city of Everett, Massachusetts, located just outside Boston. I came from a hardworking blue-collar family with strong values and a moral center. My dad worked long hours as a U.S. postal worker and custodian for the City of Everett. My mom worked just as hard at home as a housewife.

Playing and watching sports were a major part of my life as an adolescent. As a youngster, the hometown Boston Celtics were the dominant team in basketball, and the Boston Bruins had just won a pair of Stanley Cups spearheaded by a young superstar defenseman named Bobby Orr, and my idol, goaltender Gerry Cheevers.

I loved hockey and began playing at a young age. I loved the competition, winning, and even practicing.

When I reached high school, I played varsity soccer and track my sophomore year to stay in shape for hockey. By my junior year, I was considered one of the top two goaltenders in all of New England and one of the top 20 in the country. I was the #1 goalie at Hockey Nights in Boston and received honorable mention for the All-Scholastic Team.

I loved playing hockey and compiled wonderful memories over the years, but I had a burning passion for weight training. By having so much experience with the weights during my early years as a youth, I was well equipped to excel at the collegiate level.

After high school, I made a decision to concentrate on power-lifting. So, I left one sport and excelled at another, winning multiple New England competitions, including the NASA drug-free nationals.

Salem State took notice of my successes, and as a result, I became the first ever powerlifter to represent the school. It was an honor and clear indication of the school's confidence in my abilities.

The university gave me a budget to travel and enter competitions. I was the first student in the school's history to have been afforded that opportunity.

I shined in the gym. I was one place away from being an All-American at the Collegiate Nationals as a junior, with only 2 years of powerlifting experience under my belt.

I never stopped training with weights. I began at a very young age and continued on through college and to the present day.

I graduated with a bachelor's in physical education with a minor in biology. I became a physical education teacher right out of school at the junior high and high school level in my hometown of Everett, Massachusetts. I taught a subject that I was passionate about; and I'd been there, so I knew the importance of fitness and physical health for young kids.

Immediately, I noticed the differences in what did and did not work for my students, especially in regard to the way they responded to a good workout regimen. The hard workers were always on time and always alert in my class and in others. The not-so-hard workers showed me less. I saw the disparities in their motivation, lifestyles, and academic performances. But I knew there was a formula that could help each kid; it was just a matter of finding one. I would later dis-cover the formula to be weight training.

In the interim, I would coach junior high basketball and continue to train professional and amateur athletes in the gym.

Time did not allow me to give my all to my passion, so I left my teaching job and became an entrepreneur. I designed my own line of weight belts (Cardillo Weight Belts), and they quickly became the #1 custom weight belts in the world. Because of my successes in the industry, Reebok would entrust me to construct and implement a pump technique for Reebok Weight Belts. I remained with the company as a consultant and president of Reebok Weight Belts, focusing on modernization of products.

I was truly devoted to the industry, and I could concentrate on it 100 percent. In the years preceding, I had invented a revolutionary water bucket workout routine, where water gradually descends out of buckets while sets are being performed. The purpose of the exercise is to maximize muscle and cardiovascular endurance by performing a set until the point of failure, as the water gradually empties out of a small circular hole on each side of the buckets.

In 1996, I would open a sports nutrition store in Everett, Massachusetts, with my nephew, Peter Morel. Since then, our establishment has become the top single standing retail outfit for sports nutrition in the United States.

Through my experiences training with weights as a youth, I developed the tools to become a champion in life.

In the chapter titled "Peter Morel's Story: The Making of a Champion," you'll see how my nephew, an average youth, adopted my ideals and became a champion as well.

Me in my teens...

Me in my 20's...

Me in my 30's...

Me in my 40's

Unofficial World Record 1350

Me deadlifing with Howie Hoffman *(former teenage National Powerlifting Champion)* – and in my opinion pound for pound the strongest person in the world in his day!

Exhibition

Me deadlifing with my longtime training partner Andy Hickey *(former power lifting, body building and strongman champion)*

Me and Randy

Me training with my good friend Randy Savage in Tampa, Florida.

Introduction

"I wish I had this book as a youth, growing up in Canada playing hockey. It's innovative, insightful, and inspiring. I've never seen anything like it.

"My grandson, Jonathan, is 11. He's a defenseman for his youth hockey team. I gave this book to him knowing if he follows the ideals set forth, it'll pay dividends for him on the ice, as well as in his everyday life."

—Gerry Cheevers
NHL Hall of Fame Goaltender, Boston Bruins

The purpose of this book is to equip the parent, guardian, uncle, coach, or teacher with a detailed, concise, and contemporary understanding of what weight training and nutrition is, what it can and can't do, and how it can be used to aid young male adolescents in all aspects of life. This book encourages adolescent boys and young men to understand their own bodies and discover any physical or emotional limitations that might stand in the way of their goals—both on and off the field.

Even if your son falls short of his goals in the gym or on the field, this book will enable him to build a strong foundation for the rest of his life, and will undoubtedly give him the tools to become a champion in whatever it is he embarks on in his future.

I'll demonstrate through text and illustrations each body part and explain what he needs to do to get the most out of his workout safely and productively.

The same goes for his diet. He can eat right, but is he putting the right nutrients into his system to get the most out of what he's striving to accomplish on the field or in the gym? I'll present a diet plan and show how good nutrition complements good training.

A lot has changed over the years; the supplements, equipment, and ideology have all evolved together. However, my dedication to the game has never wavered. And after working with three generations of weight lifters and a number of professional and amateur athletes, I have experienced plenty of trial and error. As a result, I have fine-tuned my approach to create the best formula for success.

Through my many years of experience, teaching, and love of training, I feel I have become an expert in the field of teenage weight training. I'd like to share this knowledge with you in the hopes your son or mentee will get the most out of weight training the way I did.

You need to be there with your son every step of the way en route to his better life. Why not encourage him through weight training? The benefits could last a lifetime—and someday he'll thank you.

So, kudos to you for taking the first step toward transforming your son into a champion.

I waited 25 years to write this book. I had to wait, to see my nephew become a champion in life, so I could then show the world how it was done. Moreover, I needed to complete a full cycle on my own, carrying out my ideals to show that this works. As a person in his midlife years, I can honestly say I'm in better physical condition now than when I was a teenager, and it was all due to the work I put in at a young age. Now I have the pleasure of watching my nephew take it to a new level.

I have been truly inspired by Peter's progress as a human being and a winner. I've also been touched by the hundreds of parents and thousands of student athletes who have approached me over the years, seeking the knowledge to better their child's health through weight training.

My goal today is to take what I have retained in my ventures and relay them to a much broader group, especially to the parents who want to see their teenagers grow into well-adjusted, educated, well-mannered professional human beings. I often use the term "son" throughout the book to refer to these teenagers. But this book is not just for parents; it is truly meant for anyone carrying the responsibility of guardianship over a young adult, whether it is an uncle, coach, trainer, gym teacher, or big brother.

Knowledge is the key, and it's that awareness I give to you now.

1 | The Cardillo Way

"It wasn't always easy, and I didn't always like it, but my uncle Steve Cardillo taught me I could be successful on and off the court if I worked hard and dedicated myself in the gym.

"Through weight training, I developed the drive to want to be the best in anything I did. Today, I'm a successful businessman, and it's all due to my uncle and the virtues he instilled in me when I was a young boy."

—Peter Morel
President of American Nutrition Center
www.americannutritioncenter.com

The Cardillo Way is simply defined: *Work on all facets of your craft but give a little extra to your one true strength as it is your best asset that defines you, that makes you unique.*

When I graduated college, I realized I needed to focus on my career. Playing hockey had become a thing of the past and power-lifting had been downgraded to intense weight training. Nevertheless, I wanted to maximize my efforts in the gym with an eye toward looking better and maintaining a healthy lifestyle. (Most people I know who put athletics, or competitive weight training behind us after college, fall into this category!)

As we'll discuss in the chapter titled "Bodybuilding," most people you see in the gym have flaws. I'm no different. My calves are weaker than any other body part I train. Over the years, I have worked my calves hard, every day, and saw few or no real results. A lot of people save an extra 10–15 minutes at the end of their workout session to hit one more exercise; this gives their weaker limbs a little *oomph* in the hopes they will catch up to the stronger ones. I tried doing that. It didn't work. So I created my own philosophy: The Cardillo Way.

Whether you're an athlete, bodybuilder, musician, accountant, laborer, or actor, this principle applies to you. Here's why. The Cardillo Way preaches the fine-tuning of all facets of your game, but gives a little extra attention to your strongest asset, thus increasing your chance of success.

For example, a singer has a particular vocal range for which he's comfortable. But when he goes outside his range, he can't handle the extreme highs and lows. So instead of giving another 10–15 minutes of practice each day singing outside his range, he is best suited by working on staying within his range. This is where his true, or real, strength lies. By focusing on his true strength, he won't put himself in a position to fail. He will succeed by exploiting his strongest attribute.

Though the song bird should define himself by sticking to his true strength, it's important that he never neglects practicing out of his range on occasion; he must stay sharp.

The Cardillo Way in the gym is to train every body part, but save that extra 10–15 minutes at the end to burn your best asset. My arms respond well when I train them intensely, so I exploit that asset. As a result, my arms are truly my most positive feature.

Consider this: If a person gives 100 percent to his weaker asset, he'll get about a 10 percent return on his investment. If he gives 100 percent to his strongest asset, he'll receive about 80 percent on his investment.

Here's an example from the court.

Shaquille O'Neal will go down as one of the best big men in NBA history, but you wouldn't know it if you paid attention to his free throw shooting. He spent hours after practice trying to improve his shot from the line but made little progress. His entire career, from end to end, was terrible at the stripe. But during the flow of the game, he was nearly unstoppable around the basket.

If Shaq had adopted The Cardillo Way, he would not have practiced his free throws any more than most players. He would have spent the extra time working on his inside game to become even more dominant. If he had, he might have gone down as the best center in NBA history.

Of course, 10–15 minutes can be an extra hour for some. There are no limits.

2 | The Top Ten Components of a Champion

"Training as a young person gives someone a leg up on the competition around him. It's every kid's dream to play professional ball, and that dream should start early. A lot of people look back and ask themselves what they could have done more to go to college for free or get to the next level of their career. It always comes back to training hard and getting in that weight room.

"Aside from the weights, I cannot put enough emphasis on having the right attitude along the way. It's an extremely important component to possess, and one that can't be taught. When you're part of a team, having the right attitude will most certainly put you ahead of the pack.

"There are a lot of guys in the NFL that have natural ability but let their attitudes get in the way of their potential. It's a coach's nightmare. They would prefer the guy that listens up, that can be coached because the attitude is where it should be."

—Martin Bibla
NFL Atlanta Falcons, Denver Broncos
All-Big East 2001 Miami Hurricanes

To better understand how successful my nephew would be as an athlete, I evaluated how many components he possessed, and how each one would impact him on the field, on the court, or in his daily life. Peter didn't possess all the components, but he made up for it in other areas. For example, he had the drive, the heart, and the physical ability. He was a fighter. He fought until the end, until the buzzer sounded. He never left anything on the field or court.

Below are the components essential to becoming a champion on and off the field.

Dedication

Your son wants to make it to the next level? He better be dedicated every step of the way. There are some, unfortunately, who are so talented, have so much athleticism that they can lay down the desire to be better and can still perform at the highest level. There are so very few of them out there, but they *are* out there.

But what is dedication? It's a devotion sparked by the desire to be the best you can be, in whatever sport or activity you partake in.

See the guy who swings a baseball bat a few hundred times, the one chest deep in a swimming pool or the ocean so he can develop more bat speed? He has dedication.

See his teammate, watching from afar, getting a suntan? He lacks dedication.

But that's okay. The first guy has set different goals for himself, whereas his teammate has something else going on. Just don't count on the suntanner outslugging his teammate anytime soon.

Athleticism

Athleticism is the ability to maintain coordination while participating in a physical activity and demonstrating agility and flexibility. If he can handle all this, he's an athlete.

It's that simple. The last guy on the bench, the twelfth man on his hoop team, or even the guy the coach puts in when the game is so out of reach, is still an athlete. He might not be as athletic as the rest of the bunch, but to a degree, he has athleticism.

But, there are those who show no signs at all of any athletic ability whatsoever. It's not a horrible thing, and it certainly doesn't mean those individuals can't train with weights or compete at some level.

Attitude

Make no mistake about it. A good attitude is an extension of dedication. Don't have your son leave home without it. When he does, he's hurting himself and his team. His coach looks for the guy with the positive outlook, the one who takes direction, hustles, and sets a good example.

Coaches will take a player under their wing if they feel the athlete has the right attitude. And college recruiters and scouts will always ask the coach, "What's his attitude like?" This is because at the collegiate level, talent equals out, and if a teenager has a lousy attitude, he's replaceable.

Just remember, it's not colorful to be bad, it's stupid. Tell your son this—or his playing time will be compromised.

Physical Maturity

My nephew had success early as an athlete, but only as a result of his dedication to weight training. Physically, he was average at best until he reached his later teen years.

But it helps to have physical maturity, especially if your son matures a shade quicker than everyone else in his age group. He will have the opportunity to dominate early and often. If he continues to grow and mature, his options may change, or open up, depending on his outlook. That is, a teenager who reaches a height of 6 feet 5 inches, and weighs upwards of 250 pounds, can picture himself an offensive lineman for a football team or a center for his high school basketball squad. At this height, depending on his weight, he could be suited to participate in almost any sport if he has the talent and/or athletic ability.

However, an individual who reaches a maximum height of 5 feet 6 inches, and weighs in the vicinity of 180 pounds, will never, ever become an offensive lineman for any organization that hands out paychecks to play for them.

But the smaller guy has plenty of other options. Most skilled positions require speed and quickness, and do not necessarily need a great big build to go along with it. A few positions include defensive backs or wide receivers in football, middle infielders in baseball, and some positions in hockey, such as center and goaltender.

Danny Woodhead, running back for the New England Patriots, is listed at 5 feet 7, yet he's cemented himself as a weapon for Tom Brady and the offense coming out of the back field.

Jon Gruden, one of the NFL's best head coaches, had this to say about Danny Woodhead during a Monday Night football telecast. "... This guy represents hope for all of the kids back home who want to play pro football. This guy's 5 feet 7. He comes from a small college. He's 180 pounds, and he's starting for the New England Patriots. Keep lifting weights back home, kids."

Dustin Padroia of the Boston Red Sox, Brian Giaonta of the Montreal Canadiens, and Wes Welker of the New England Patriots are all considered undersized compared to the rest of the competition. All three are great talents, and all have had a great deal of success by settling into positions that allow them to get the most out of their abilities.

So it helps to know where your teenager stacks up in his later teen years. Once you figure that out, the direction becomes clear.

If your son happens to be held back a year in elementary school for academic or social reasons, think of it as a positive. He'll be more mature physically in athletics, and that's not a bad thing.

Mental Toughness

Only the strong survive. And without mental toughness, it'll be difficult to stay alive. With mental toughness comes confidence. But let's not confuse confidence with cockiness.

Cockiness is telling a coach and anyone within an earshot that he's going to make the big play; but in his mind, he's really not sure. He's more afraid than anything. He's rolling the dice.

A confident person wants to make the big play, and usually does. Fear does not enter the equation, only mental toughness does.

The answers a teenager looks for come from within. So he needs to ask himself, is he the guy who wants the ball hit in his direction or wants to take the last shot?

He's the guy who can't wait to get the ball back, because he knows in his 2-minute drill, he's going to march his team down the field for the winning score. Is *this* your son? He has "it," right?

If not, it's okay, and realizing it will help him out more than you think. If he passes up the last shot to someone more capable or asks to not be involved in the critical points in the game, he's giving his team a better shot to win.

What about when he's ready to play at the next level?

From high school to college, or college to the pros, there are significant adjustments he'll need to make to ensure a smooth transition. He'll need to come to grips with a lot of change. For example, he'll make new friends. His coach isn't the same person, and he's not the same player; he may no longer be the #1 guy. For some, it's easy. For others, it's not. He'll have to show some level of mental toughness to get by.

Same goes for that person who plays in the corporate world. New coworkers. New boss. New position, perhaps? Maybe even a new strategy or game plan? It's all relative. But at the same time, he has to keep a certain level of mental toughness. If he does, his odds of becoming a champion in some aspect of life will go up.

Heart

What is heart?

Well, it's one's last resort; when the game is on the line, he reaches for that last bit of physical or mental energy he can muster to make it to the Promised Land. It's when he pushes himself to that place he has never been before, because he wants victory that bad.

We see it in boxers when they refuse to go down; football players when they have little or no energy left but manage to find a shred of force and make a play; or a goaltender who's gassed, who just stopped 40 shots in Game 7 and is asked to continue on in overtime—and he does.

It's asking yourself to try one more time when you're seemingly out of gas. It's rejuvenating yourself emotionally when you've hit a wall physically.

That's what heart is.

It's another component, or intangible, that can't be taught. Like the rest of these components, there are different levels.

Having heart is quite a weapon in all aspects of life.

Coach-ability

Coach-ability goes hand-in-hand with attitude. A teenager who wants to be coached is welcoming constructive criticism so he can become better at what he does. A coach would rather embrace a teenager who is open to criticism and is coachable over a teenager who is very talented but uncoachable. A coach is more likely to give him more chances to succeed, even if the teenager lacks most of the components listed here.

Your teenager should be showing his coach he wants to learn. If he does, he's a winner. He's only going to better himself, and at the same time, he'll be setting a great example for his teammates. He's becoming a leader without even knowing it.

This is why the captain of the team is not always the most talented individual, but he's almost always a great leader. This goes for organized team sports on all levels.

Success begins with coach-ability and a positive attitude.

Leadership Ability

It's about being confident, composed, and driven. It's about having great discipline and commanding respect from his team. It's about having enthusiasm, being selfless, and sacrifice. An effective leader puts his ego and self-image on the back burner and focuses on the well-being of his team. If your son possesses these qualities, he is, or is well on his way to becoming, a great leader.

By being a leader, he's making his team better. Great leaders have the courage to point out what went wrong, what went right, and they have the ability to delegate responsibility so everyone understands the common goal—winning!

For some, it comes naturally. For others, it's a matter of leaving their comfort zone, stepping up, and appointing themselves the guy who's taking control.

Your son can get there if he wants to. Show him the way!

For more on leadership, check out our chapter titled "Pat Downey, Life and Leadership."

Character

If your son has great character, he has a prominent worth about him. He likely leads by example and can oftentimes harvest a following without even trying.

He's the silent chief. He leads by example on and off the field, utilizing a great moral inner core and projects himself with class and respect.

He's the guy who's thorough, always on time, and shows commitment. He's trusting, motivated, and always looking to improve his game.

A great character guy goes a long way in transforming a team that lacks a respectable self-image to a group of guys who portray honor and decency from the water boy to the head coach.

His traits can be contagious, if you let them be.

Natural Talent

It's the number-one component. Does your son have it? If he does, where did it come from?

Natural talent is a gift, afforded to him the day he was born. It's not something he can learn. If it wasn't there the day he was brought into this world, he'll never have it because it's not something he can develop over time.

My nephew wasn't the most talented individual on his feet, as discussed, but made up for it with weight training. He also had an uncanny way of dedicating himself to his goals.

Most people, however, are born with different levels of talent. For example, let's use musicians. Two beginners pick up a saxophone the same day, learn the same lessons, and put in the exact same amount of effort, yet one seems to pick it up a little easier than the other. The one that's ahead has more talent, and the other has to work harder at it to catch up.

However, one can develop skills, such as more bat speed, better form on skates, or a sweeter stroke with a basketball. A lot of skills can be picked up by weight training. No one could box out opponents under the basket like my nephew could because he was so strong.

Now, have you ever heard someone say, "He does things that can't be taught . . . ?" Well, what someone can't teach is talent. But not having much talent doesn't mean your son can't play a sport or get involved in athletic activities. He can still be an athlete.

Take Daniel "Rudy" Rudiger, the real-life gentleman depicted in the motion picture *Rudy*. Don't let anyone kid you; this guy was talented, but talented enough to make it to the NFL? No. But he had enough skills to play for a Division I powerhouse (powerhouse at the time) like Notre Dame. Why? Because he had more heart, will, and desire than anyone in the state of Indiana. That's what got him to that level. He was an athlete.

Joe Montana was one of the best quarterbacks we've ever seen play on Sundays. He was picked in the third round of the NFL draft because he wasn't as talented as the quarterbacks selected before him—so the masses thought. He would become a four-time Super Bowl champion. He was every bit as talented as anyone else; he was just overlooked for reasons we can't explain.

Martin St. Louis of the NHL's Tampa Bay Lightning went undrafted but would still be awarded the MVP of the Stanley Cup finals in 2008.

Kurt Warner, one of the NFL's most clutch quarterbacks of his era, was stocking shelves when he signed with the St. Louis Rams. In his first full season with the Rams, Warner would lead his team to a Super Bowl championship. He was never drafted.

Of course, who can forget basketball's greatest player of all time, Michael Jordan? He was cut from his varsity high school basketball team but would later become the world's best.

It happens.

Try to evaluate your son's level of talent. It's important, and doing it correctly can determine whether you're putting him in a position to succeed.

The Good News

The good news is that whether you have all or none of the required components to make it as a champion, you'll always have weight training to excel at. You will, because your resources are nearly endless. You have the gym, your basement . . . or you can simply improvise using an array of exercises available in every direction. You just have to look for them.

3 | Fallacies and Misconceptions about Weight Training

"Training with weights early in my life enabled me to set goals, become a confident leader, not only on the field, but in the classroom . . . and when I reached my growth spurt around 13-14, I hit the ground running, all because I learned the fundamentals of weight training at an early age."

—Dan Curran
NFL—Seattle Seahawks, New Orleans Saints
Arena Football League—Nashville Kats,
Georgia Force, New Orleans VooDoo

Myth #1
Weight training stunts your growth

When I was a gym teacher, I always encountered parents who had questions about their child's behavior, performance in class, or their overall, physical well-being. But the most common question was, "Will [lifting weights] stunt my child's growth?"

I believe the answer is no!

I've been weight training for the better part of my life, and I started as a young teen. I stand a mere 5 feet 8 inches. I'm in great shape, but because of my broadness, most people think I am short. The truth is, I'm the tallest one in my family!

We're all coded with DNA, and it's that code that determines our growth potential. It's my opinion that through exercising and eating properly you can increase your chances of reaching your full growth potential because both components stimulate growth.

Does this mean there is a chance you could exceed your growth potential by exercising and keeping up with an impeccable diet? No one really knows the answer to that.

I do believe if you're going to isolate one factor, you should take a look at what your children eat instead of what they lift over their heads.

But let's take this into consideration: Before the turn of the twentieth century, the average person was considerably smaller than the average person of today. Soldiers in the military, in particular, would be overpowered in hand-to-hand combat versus the modern-day warrior. Why is that?

The physical training endured by soldiers today is far more rigorous and intense than the routines our grandfathers were put through. Also, modern-day soldiers have diets that are much sounder than the rations served up in the trenches more than a half century ago.

I monitored my nephew Peter's diet and ensured that, in addition to his weight training routine, he received the right nutrients—and at 6 foot 2, I believe he did!

Ignore all the misconceptions. If your boy eats right and exercises, his chances of living up to his full growth potential are greatly increased.

Myth #2
Weight training makes you muscle bound

Not likely.

Weight training, when performed correctly, involves the complete motion of a particular muscle group through its full range. Weight training that is performed properly means that your muscles will grow and become more defined and more flexible. If your range of motion surrenders, and your flexibility becomes compromised, then you are not weight training correctly. Or, the reason may be simple—you cheated by taking some sort of anabolic or methylated product.

We all see them. It's a classmate, a coworker, or just a bystander at the local market; you can pick them out of a crowd because they're simply bigger and more defined than the rest. They have a hard time putting their arms behind their heads or shooting a basketball.

Truth be told, the only reason they do look awkward throwing or shooting a ball is because they never knew how to in the first place. They may have chosen weight training because it requires very little natural athletic ability.

Becoming apprehensive about weight training or strength and conditioning out of fear of getting "too big" is just plain silly. The idea undoubtedly should be put out of your child's mind. The health benefits are too important to ignore!

Myth #3
Muscle turns into fat

This would be the equivalent of turning apples into oranges, or silver into gold. It can't happen.

People who weight train take in an excess amount of calories, or more calories than their body is accustomed to consuming regularly. When they call it quits or simply tone down the workouts, and if they continue the same caloric intake, it's only natural for their muscles to slowly decrease in size, while a nice layer of fat develops on top. The transformation is happening all in one motion, or concurrently, so it appears the muscle is turning into fat.

However, if they continue to eat properly and consume the correct amount of protein to feed the muscle, there won't be any layer of fat covering the muscle.

Myth #4
Your child will get hurt by weight training

They'll get hurt jumping off a diving board if no one taught them how to land safely in the water, too. They'll get hurt launching a shot put in the air—if no one taught them the proper technique.

If this myth were true, then why do people with injuries use weights to rehabilitate themselves? For example, even in extreme cases (like after surgery), the patient will need to exercise with weights to bring back strength to the muscle affected by the procedure.

Weight training injuries occur when a person pushes himself too hard, does not use the proper techniques, or trains while unsupervised. All three are a recipe for disaster.

As long as you take the necessary precautions while overseeing your teenager's weight training, sustaining an injury is highly unlikely. I always took precautions with my nephew, and as a result, he never got hurt.

Myth #5
Weight training will increase your child's athletic talent

Not likely. If you think weight training will make him go from having two left feet to acquiring a one-way ticket straight to the pros, think again. He's either born with talent, or he's not. Weight training will not necessarily increase his talent.

That said, it's true that exercise can improve his overall strength, flexibility, range of motion, endurance, and stamina. This will make him a better overall athlete and can usually lead to more production on the field as well.

A great example is Billy Wagner, a former left-handed major league baseball reliever. Wagner was listed at 5 feet 11 inches and weighed just over 200 pounds. He had a slight build for a pitcher, but when he reared back, he could throw a ball 100 mph! I have seen guys in high school and college with much bigger builds (well over 6 feet tall with wide frames) that couldn't break 80 mph on the radar gun. So how could someone as small as Billy Wagner perform this feat?

It's because Billy Wagner was born with a great talent, or gift! I'm sure he worked hard as well, and at one time had to adjust his mechanics to add a few miles per hour to his fastball, but only a few.

The same goes for the senior in high school that tops out at 70 mph off a mound. With the proper mechanics, he could raise his fastball another 4–6 mph, but there's no way he'll ever be able to throw close to 90 mph. It just won't happen. He simply does not possess the talent.

The same goes for the frail kid turned muscle bound—the added muscle won't turn him into superman. He'll just look bigger when he throws a baseball.

The point is that through proper diet and exercise, a boy will increase his production on the field, but it will never raise his talent level.

Just the same, it's important for boys to recognize the benefits of hard work and dedication in any activity, because without them, it becomes very difficult to make it in anything, let alone sports. And he just might have the opportunity to blow away the other kid with the talent.

4 | Why Weight Restrictions Fail Our Youth

"A proper strength and conditioning program is essential for any young athlete these days. The competition is so fierce that maximizing your physical fitness greatly enhances your chance of succeeding.

"I started training at a very young age. It is one of the major assets that has helped me excel and achieve my goals of playing at the collegiate and professional levels."

—Jason Krog
NHL New York Islanders, Mighty Ducks of Anaheim, New York Rangers, Vancouver Canucks
Hobey Baker Memorial Award—1999

There is no more important time in a person's life with respect to nutrition and growth than between the time of birth to the age of 18. In no way should your child restrict proper nutrients during these years, unless a doctor gives explicit instructions, i.e., if someone is overweight or has some sort of physical ailment. Otherwise, diet restriction should never happen.

I made sure, to the best of my ability, that my nephew received the proper nutrients as a kid. It was common sense to me. I felt anything less would compromise his overall health and physical maturation process.

A lot of people are concerned with their son overtraining, but what they really should worry about is their son undereating.

The two biggest culprits responsible for influencing a youngster to hold back on a proper diet are youth football and high school wrestling. These are two activities I felt Peter could have competed in during his advanced stages as a teenage weight trainer. However, participating in these sports would have required him to manipulate his weight by depriving himself of nutrients, and I'd have none of it.

The alternative was to play basketball and soccer. This way, he could maintain his speed and agility and mature physically at the same time.

Youth Football

Youth football has strict rules about determining what level the youth is most suited for, and the main variable is his weight class. For example, if a youth at an early age, let's say 11, happens to be a mountain among molehills compared to his peers, he has but one option if he wants to throw the pads on and play: he needs to lose weight. This requires him to cut back on the calorie intake in the hopes he can make the weight class and join the squad.

Just as harmful is the 14-year-old who is entering high school early; he might drop his weight to 110 pounds so that he can still play at a pre-high school level—and perhaps dominate the competition due to his mental maturity and football experience.

There couldn't be a worse resolution in wanting to play ball at a high level. By restricting diet and exercise, youths run the risk of negatively impacting their growth potential. They should be upping the calorie intake, especially the protein, if they are involved in activities other than weight training.

If you have a son in this predicament—he's simply too big to play at a certain level, and he's forced to either sit out or play with the older teenagers with more experience that probably hit a lot harder as well. Here's my advice: Sit the teenager out.

Why?

Why have him be subjected to the beating? Let your son weight train and eat right to keep him on the fast track to his maximum growth potential. If you feel he has natural athletic ability, you might as well wait until high school to let him play again. He'll be growing natural muscle rather than losing it, and won't be taking a beating at the same time.

By the time he reaches high school, there's a good chance he'll be stronger, thus, making him more equipped to handle the physical contact. He'll also already have a good understanding of the game because he watched plenty of games on TV, and he practiced the skilled positions on his own time at the park with his friends. He may have spent time in the backyard throwing a football around with his father or family friend, too. Also, he doesn't have to start his freshman year in high school. He could begin later if he wants. Don't rush him.

Why else do NFL organizations at times look to Olympic athletes, or basketball players, or speed skaters to sign someone? Because they know these individuals possess either the speed or athletic ability to make it in the NFL.

Still not convinced?

On January 17, 2009, the TV show *60 Minutes* ran a story about the diminutive rock island of Samoa, located in a vast, stand-alone region of the South Pacific. The island harbors roughly 65,000 residents of Samoa; more than 30 of which play ball for an NFL team. That's a ratio of around 2000:1, citizens to professional football players.

Astounding!

It's even more so, considering the odds of an American-born player making it to the NFL is less than a tenth of a percent!

What's also remarkable is that Samoans weren't introduced to youth football until 2009. So these 30 athletes never played a down of football until they got to high school. Rather than taking a physical beating as a preteen, Samoans hit the shoddy weight rooms and rock-infested fields to develop their skills.

And Samoans are big; they believe in hard work, respect, strength, and discipline. It's because of these ideals that Samoan-born males are 56 times more likely to make it to the NFL than American-born men.

So if you can, don't rush your teenager onto the field if you don't have to. Let him grow and build muscle—because phase two will come that much easier.

High School Wrestling

Starving your son of food to drop weight is bad, but depriving him of liquids as well is just unacceptable. Unfortunately, this is a practice all too common in high school wrestling.

High school wrestlers are often motivated to lose weight in the hopes of competing in a specific weight class. But these athletes are flirting with disaster in the name of dehydration.

A young man's body is made up of mostly water for a reason. Water makes the organs function properly. Depriving him of water can only spell bad news, especially for a teenager. Dehydration can cause muscle cramps, dizziness, headaches, and in extreme cases, death.

Though your teenager may be in seemingly good physical condition, there is no doubt that by limiting his consumption of nutrients and dehydrating him, it will lead to a drop in production on the mat.

So what you have is a catch-22 at its core. He's dropping the weight and qualifying for a weight class, but he's less effective when he's competing as a result.

The same theory applies in wrestling as it does in youth football. Instead of depriving your youth of the basic building blocks to gain muscle, you should be making every attempt to add the muscle by encouraging weight training and a high protein intake. If he's good enough and has the talent, the people at the next level will notice—no matter what weight class he competes in. And if and when he does make it to the next level, he can begin to play around with his weight through a sound diet and nutrition plan.

Now, what happens when he refuses to lose the weight, thus causing animosity to build between him and his coach? It's sad, but the guy calling the shots has a lot of influence on where he'll compete the following season, whether it's in high school, or at a college, or university. His life can change with one phone call to a college coach or recruiter. That's a lot of pressure on a young fellow trying to make it in this world, pressure we hope we can help him scrap eventually.

5 | The Benefits of Weight Training and Exercise

"I began training with weights in seventh-grade in my basement. I played three sports: football, basketball, and baseball. In order to play all three sports well, I knew I had to improve my speed, strength, and agility. I lifted weights because my older brother Scott did, and he was 5 years older than me. Like Scott, I knew the more strength I gained, the faster and more flexible I would become and the better I would play—so I hit the gym early and often.

"As I began to excel on the football field and baseball diamond, I gained more confidence in life, and it carried over into my schoolwork. My improved self-esteem can be attributed to my increased physical maturity training with weights in my basement. I loved working hard, and it paid off when I played sports. Playing better in sports was important to me. I knew that training hard would put me ahead of the other boys my age because Scott became captain of the high school baseball and football team, and I knew his extra weight training helped him be a leader.

"I was self-motivated and took pride in working hard behind the scenes. The work I put in made me proud of my accomplishments but kept me grounded. I always strived to get better physically, and it mentally gave me an edge over my competition. I believed that training at an early age gave me an advantage over my peers, and is why I believe 100 percent in what I do for a living—Performance Training for People's Goals!"

—Pete Ohnegian
Strength & Conditioning Coach, former professional football player
www.goodenergytraining.com

Below are examples of some of the basic returns your son will receive when he incorporates weight training and other exercise activities into his life.

Build Confidence

Your child can experience a lot of positive changes in his life if he improves his appearance. And there is no more critical time in his life to do so than when he becomes a teenager. This was certainly the case with my nephew Peter.

He may want to shed some weight, tone his muscles, or gain a little size; whatever the case may be, once he begins to see the difference, his confidence will undergo a dramatic change—a positive change—all because of his hard work.

It's a beautiful time in a youngster's life.

Having this newfound self-esteem is the key to success in his teen years, and even interacting in social settings will become a little easier. It's that self-esteem that breeds confidence. Being confident can pay dividends in most facets of life.

For instance, if your son is sitting across from a seemingly daunting figure, such as a job interviewer, it can be a scary thing. But when he speaks eloquently, and with conviction, while maintaining strong eye contact, this will make a positive difference for him. It might also allow him to stand out among most young men of his age.

These are just two examples, but having confidence will take your teenager to many places in life worth visiting, and he'll likely encounter positive results in anything he sets his mind to doing.

Boost Energy Level

Giving your teenager an extra push on a daily basis could prove to be highly beneficial and often results in the domino effect: The more you encourage him, the more he improves. That's what weight training and exercise can do for him.

It all begins with a good night's sleep. Getting enough shut-eye to power him through the long days of school is essential, and the rewards can be plentiful. He will wake up refreshed and ready to take on anything, including those pesky pop quizzes we've all grown to dislike through the years.

He will become more alert, and his class participation (a component which often determines his final grade) will improve immensely. His answers will be clearer, more concise, and on target. He'll absorb more knowledge and be ready for the next algebra exam.

Although overcoming his learning disability was an uphill battle, Peter still gave his all to his studies, eventually earning his high school degree. Without weight training and athletics in his life, his motivation may have suffered. Instead, he strived to be the best and overcame the odds. Imagine what your son can do, especially if he is not hindered by a disability.

Keep the Blood Flowing Continuously throughout the Day

Can he walk to school? If he can, go for it, and have him walk home as well. If not, have him wait for his lunch break or study hall, and get outside and walk on the track; encourage him to stay active. This will keep his body and mind from wanting to rest his head on a pillow. You don't want to be the parent of the teenager who falls asleep in class. It might give your teenager's friends a good laugh, but in the long run, he will look like a fool—and will not gain the teacher's respect.

Grow in the Workplace

After school he might have a job. He may dread it (we all did), but teens like to have a little money in their pockets; and it's good for parents to see their progress, too. If they have that extra spring in their step and a little discipline, their job performance will increase, thus, giving them the opportunity to move up the company ladder and make more money. He may only be delivering pizza, but doing it well and earning a raise does wonders for his self-confidence.

Professionally, being more confident in the workplace goes a long way. Your child will be less afraid to speak up and will likely become a superb decision maker. It's that type of behavior that employers and future employers look for. The kind of behavior that spells p-r-o-m-o-t-i-o-n!

Benefit from Chores

If he doesn't have a job, there's a good chance you, the parent, are putting him to work around the house in the form of chores. Is there anything worse for him?

But if he's exercising daily, the chores such as mowing the lawn, raking the leaves, or taking out the trash become easier, more manageable physically, and of course, less time-consuming. He may even begin to enjoy the chores if he feels he's benefiting on a fitness level.

Why not try to make the chores more beneficial to him? Here are a few tips:

- Garbage and recycling removal. If he's taking out the trash and recycling, make sure the weight is distributed evenly as he walks to the curb.
- Painting. Instruct him on how to paint the house, painting half the house with his right arm and the other half with his left arm.
- Lawn mowing. Have him wear a weight vest or a heavy backpack when he mows the lawn.
- Raking. Encourage him to rake the leaves—half on his right side and half on his left.

These are just a few examples. I'm sure you can create more for your son. Be creative, and always keep a cautious eye on what he's doing. If it doesn't appear safe, stay away from it.

Look Better

Looking better and feeling better about his self-image will undoubtedly set him on a path to improving his social life. This will bring him to another level—a responsible one, hopefully.

Encouragement is a powerful force. I encouraged my nephew, and it paid off. It was a strong motivator.

So tell your son how good he looks. Receiving encouragement from you will motivate your child and make him feel better on the inside because his "inner hero" is appreciating the results.

Once more, he will see a difference in the mirror almost daily. As a teenager, his body is changing every day anyway. Add in a weight training regimen to complement his natural growth and his drive will come alive. The changes will propel him to continue working hard and, thus, forcing a drastic but positive change in his overall confidence.

Of course, how good he can look is impossible to answer. However, we do know that a positive transformation in appearance often opens up doors.

He'll never know what the day is going to bring him when he walks out the door. He could be at the right place, at the right time, when that right person approaches him with a job offer, just because of the way he looks.

Become Goal Oriented

Your child's commitment to goals will go a long way in determining what kind of success he can achieve in life. Whether it's in the classroom, the gym, on the ball field, at home with the teenagers, or at the office, training his mind to reach for the top helps him develop into the champion he wants to be.

When my nephew trained with weights, he was continuously setting and reaching goals. As your son trains with weights, he's doing the same. He challenges himself by adding more weight to the bar. He pushes himself to complete a few more reps (keep in mind, this mind-set is for the advanced weight trainer). He commands himself to last just a few more minutes on the treadmill.

Training his body also helps him train his mind. It will help him become an unstoppable force, a go-getter; the type of person who refuses to lose; the one who goes the extra mile to achieve a goal most people deem unattainable.

Training himself to reach for the stars cannot be stated enough.

It can work the same with his academic studies. Just 10 pages left; five pages left; one page left, and he's done. And he can complete it all by a certain time. By 5 P.M., all of his homework is going to be finished.

Why? Because now he has the energy and drive to get it done, a piece of cake. And he has left plenty of leisure time to fill before he calls it a day.

Of course, not everyone can rush home after school and immediately break out the textbooks and whale away at them. He might have sports practice or an after-school job, or some other obligation that fills his time productively. The important thing is for him to pick a time he wants to finish, and finish. Because learning to budget his time properly, all while learning how to be a goal-driven individual, is a recipe for success.

Stave Off Those Bullies

Bullies head for the weakest and most in need. When they lay their eyes on someone who's physically fit, no matter how tough the target is or is not, they seem to look the other way. It's their cowardly nature. I've seen it many times as a teacher.

If your son does happen to get in a tussle, at least he'll have some added strength, quickness, and extra stamina to get him out of the situation.

As a parent, you won't have to worry much about your teenager being the victim of bullying.

Prevent Injuries

Physical fitness or weight training will make your child stronger, more toned, and more flexible. It will also improve his balance and range of motion. All of these components prevent injuries.

We've seen it before and at all levels. When athletes report to training camp or preseason slow and out of shape, you can bet they will eventually find their way onto the disabled list at one time or another. It's just not worth it.

When your teenager is in high school, particularly his junior year, when scouts and college recruiters begin to take notice of his play on the field, it would be catastrophic for him to come up lame with an injury.

This applies to more individuals than you think. Whether a stout high school halfback, or a 30-something beer league softball player, by taking cautionary preventatives as a youth by weight training, the odds of sustaining a serious injury dramatically go down.

Training as a youth prevents injuries later in life. Plus, the healthier your son is as a child, the healthier he'll be as an adult.

But let's face it, some injuries are just unavoidable. Yet even so, it's the stronger, healthier, and physically fit individuals who seem to heal quicker than others.

Note: *Nutrition encourages and complements weight training and exercise.*

Weight training will just not do it alone. Balanced nutrition is essential and complements the results gained by exercise.

Avoid or Slow Disease

Medically speaking, here are diseases your youth is more likely to avoid—now and as an adult—by eating right and weight training as a young person.

- Childhood diabetes
- Childhood obesity

- High blood pressure
- High cholesterol
- Osteoporosis
- Depression

You'll learn more on nutrition in our chapter titled "Evaluating Your Body Type and Nutrition."

6 | Evaluating Your Body Type and Nutrition

"Kids today are timid. They lack the toughness we've grown accustomed to seeing from the youths of yesterday. Moreover, training as a young person is a way to boost the self-esteem and self-confidence, which is so crucial in one's early life development.

"The dedication to exercise and good nutrition at an early age promotes a structured lifestyle, as well as muscle growth, and undoubtedly decreases the chances of sustaining an injury."

—Mike Neu
NFL Scout

Take a good look at your son and determine what body type class he falls under. Is he a mesomorph, ectomorph, or endomorph?

Knowing the three body types and where he fits in to all of them helps determine his best course of action with respect to a balanced diet complemented by the right physical activity.

Here are brief descriptions of the three physiques, and my opinions on all.

A "mesomorph" is the best-case scenario for building muscle. A mesomorph responds better than most when consuming a balanced diet consisting of higher protein. He is what he eats. A mesomorph's physique is symmetrical, with well-defined muscle tissue and thick bone density.

An "ectomorph" is a notch below mesomorph. An ectomorph's frame is lanky, with more slender limbs and a smaller bone density. He can get away with eating the high calorie foods in an untimely fashion, but needs to regulate his diet to a degree to gain the weight. He'll need to eat, even when he doesn't want to put on the pounds.

My nephew was an ectomorph. He was a skinny kid, but he beefed through weight training.

But make no mistake, a high calorie diet consisting of an abundance of bad fats may not destroy someone on the outside so much, but it will destroy that person's insides. Not to mention the bad habits he will pick up by going down this path.

An "endomorph" has a tougher road ahead when it comes to achieving the goals outlined in this book; tougher, though not impossible. He's round with little muscle tone. And his diet must be stricter than the aforementioned mesomorph or ectomorph. An extreme endomorph responds negatively to the slightest buildup of high fat and high calorie foods. He'll require a more balanced diet with less cheating.

However, no matter what class he falls under, it's okay for him to enjoy a McDonald's cheeseburger, or a Santarpio's pizza once in awhile, as long as he stays active and keeps the balance. Keep your son conscious of what he's eating, and make sure he's eating at the right times of the day. That includes 5–6 small meals a day.

It's my opinion that if he gets the hungry horrors late at night, the most beneficial type of food to consume would be a protein shake. First, he'd be taking in a low-fat, low-calorie snack that will help build muscle. Second, your son should never go more than 8 hours without any protein intake. So keep track of what time he goes to bed and what time he gets up. At the 8-hour mark, protein consumption becomes important.

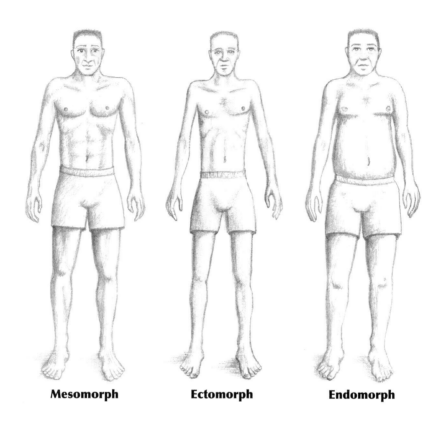

Mesomorph   **Ectomorph**   **Endomorph**

Overall Nutrition

Now, I'm not going to lay out an exotic diet chart (similar to the ones you see on every magazine cover at the checkout stand) filled with nuts and berries and all kinds of organic fluff. I could, but that only works in a perfect world, and it's expensive!

What I want to preach to you is simple: Keep his protein high, the carbs at a moderate plane, and the fat at a low level.

Protein feeds the muscle. It only makes sense that the more protein he takes in, the better chance he has of gaining muscle through weight training and exercise. Biological protein is best. Some examples of biological protein are meat, fish, eggs, and chicken.

More on Protein

I once participated in a blind protein absorption study, conducted by Tufts University, to determine at what point my body would begin to cannibalize itself based on the amount of protein I was taking in.

I can only relay to you what my experience was like. Young teenagers aren't allowed to participate in studies like this, so it's important you know I'm not making any claims here. I can only tell you that at 200 pounds, my body would require more than 75 grams of protein daily just to maintain my natural muscle, never mind what it would take to add muscle.

It depends how active your teenager is before he can determine how much protein he should take in. The more calories your son burns throughout the day, the more he'll be able to process.

The issue with these studies is that most of the time they're conducted using participants who exude little or no exercise in their daily lives. Thus, you'll hear through the wire how much protein is safe to consume based on your body weight. If you're unclear on how much protein your son should consume, seek out a physician's opinion.

Three generations of my family (my uncle, me, and my nephew) all enhanced our protein intake with powder protein. In my day, I used Hoffman Protein. It was a brand that has since stopped manufacturing protein. Protein has come a long way since Hoffman shut down.

Now, the foods I highly recommend for a great source of protein include whey protein or egg protein. Whey protein is a mixture of proteins isolated from whey in cheese. Protein is essential in building muscle, and it's the first thing that wilts away when the body doesn't have enough to digest. Egg protein is essentially egg whites, but it's also available in powder form.

However, whether we're talking about 30 years ago, or today, on a day-to-day basis, I personally find it too difficult to consume the amount of protein in solid form needed to achieve the gains we look for. It's less expensive and more convenient to drink the protein rather than eat it. These are the main reasons I'm recommending whey or egg protein.

When it comes to supplementation overall, you make the choice for your teenager. Ask yourself how aggressive you want to be with respect to giving him more alternatives. Make sure he's old enough. Most products specify a recommended age on the label.

There are a lot of great and effective products for preworkout, postworkout, and recovery. I strongly recommend you do all the research you can on them before you make the call.

The bottom line is, your son should know his own body, and what it can handle. If he's not responding well to what he eats, seek out a physician to get the answers you're looking for.

For a list of reputable companies that offer preworkout and postworkout supplements, as well as protein, check out our reference page in the back of the book.

7 | Introduction to Weight Training

"I've been training for 40 years and training young athletes for nearly 20 years. Although 9 years Steve's senior, I've looked to Steve as a training mentor. I've applied many of Steve's principles to the athletes I've trained, many of which are professional hockey players.

"I have three sons that have consistently applied the methods Steve writes about. Benn, 23, graduated from Governors Academy and went on to Boston College as a scholarship athlete, winning a national championship in 2008 with the Eagles. He is presently playing with the San Jose Sharks organization.

"Cody, 18, graduated from Governors Academy and went on to Northeastern University as a scholarship athlete. He was drafted in the 5th round of the 2010 NHL Entry Draft by the San Jose Sharks.

"Nathan, 16, is attending Governors Academy. Entering his sophomore year, Nathan recently accepted a full scholarship offer to join his brother, Cody, at Northeastern University.

"Training has been the cornerstone of their development."

—Peter Ferriero
Founder of Top Gun Youth Hockey, The Eastern Hockey
Federation, and The New England Fall Prep Hockey League
www.topgunhockey.org

The Learning Phase

As I preached to my nephew in his younger years, you'll find no more important time in your son's life than his learning phase. This is when he learns the fundamentals of weight training; it's where it all begins. It has to, because no one jumps right into anything without learning the basics, right? It's important to learn the basics first, especially if you have respect for the sport and want to be realistic about what you can do.

One thing that cannot be overstated is he must master the basics of weight training before ever thinking of experimenting with more advanced training methods, such as using chains or kettle bells. I spent a calendar year working with my nephew, teaching him the basics before anything else. I was adamant, and you should be, too.

It's common sense! Before the house comes the foundation.

Now, you've heard it on TV, when commentators refer to an athlete as being "fundamentally sound." They say it for a reason—it's important.

Learning the fundamentals in anything is experiencing something in its most basic form, making it easier for you to comprehend. The fundamentals are necessary for your teenager to build a relationship with the core of what he's trying to learn, so he can master it later in life. Fundamentals are the building blocks to success.

It's no different with weight training. He must learn to crawl, and then walk, before he could ever think of running. This is how he should approach weight training.

When to Begin

How old is he? How far along is he in his physical maturation process? Some bodies mature faster than others, and some simply lag behind. There are questions you need to answer *before* you develop a workout regimen for your son. If you can't answer some of them on your own, speak to a physician.

Otherwise, in my opinion, he should begin in his junior high school years so when he gets to high school he'll be ready to train at a higher level. He'll already have the fundamentals down, which will make for a smooth transition.

However, if he's in high school, or even older, he has to begin at the learning phase. If that's the case, he may be physically mature and can handle the exercises easier and with greater speed. For instance, where 2 years is a good time span to complete the learning phase, 1 year may suffice for the older, more physically mature individual.

Stretching

Learning to crawl begins with having a good stretching session before and after any physical activity.

Cardio

A good warm-up with cardio increases blood flow, thus giving you the energy to maximize your workout. I always felt more energized and flexible after beginning my routine with some cardio. Twenty minutes on a bike or on a run will suffice.

Always Stay Hydrated

Lesson One is simple. He must stay hydrated! To maintain optimum performance, make sure he consumes plenty of fluids during any of the routines suggested in this book. The body will lose plenty of water, and it must be replaced adequately.

The method of hydration can come in the form of water or a variety of multiflavored sports performance drinks packed with the right nutrients to keep your son's engine running on all cylinders for the duration of his activity. When he's lounging around the house, he should be consuming water.

Training Frequency

This depends on one's schedule, ability, age, and maturity. For example, most young adults have a variety of activities keeping them busy in their daily lives aside from sports, and this should be encouraged.

Your child's physical abilities may be far superior to others, or he may have some catching up to do. Whatever the case may be, each scenario will factor into his training frequency.

Weight Training Guidelines

Below is a comprehensive set of guidelines for a workout routine for him to get started with; it will allow plenty of time for you to evaluate where he stands. These routines will:

- permit enough time for recreation and
- encourage him to enjoy all the benefits of a learning phase/workout routine

Follow Sound Training Limits

Younger weight trainers especially should never go all-out for one repetition (rep). A "rep" is the complete motion of an exercise involving weights. It's as simple as that. A "set" is a collection of reps. So for instance, 10 reps is a set of 10. Five reps is a set of five, and so on.

A 10- or 15-rep limit for the first 2 years is highly recommended. A three-rep limit should only be done when an individual has reached an advanced stage closer to the age of 16. Fewer reps indicate more weight.

Do not push your son to his limits too early. The results will not be favorable. Having a three-rep limit, even if only one or two reps were completed, allows him to still accomplish something without reaching his goal. However, having a limit of one is asking for trouble. That's how injuries happen.

If an individual fights to complete one rep, the weight is simply too much. This is a practice that's shunned upon during the learning phase.

Avoid Stress

For the first couple of years, a weight trainer should not be put under any stress to accomplish anything—unless it pertains to form, rest, sleep, and nutrition. The lifter should never be pushed to uncomfortable limits that cause unnecessary fatigue.

Use a Simple Method

The method that the beginner should utilize is simple. Find a comfortable weight, and then use that weight to do four sets at 12 reps each. If that can be done successfully, without any significant strain, then increase weight an additional 5 pounds for him and have him perform the same exercise and number of reps the following workout. If he fails to reach 12 reps on one or more of his sets, then he should continue using the same weight. The weight should only be increased when he can successfully perform four sets of 12 reps without difficulty, having rested 60–90 seconds between each set.

4 sets of 12 reps each (rest 60–90 seconds between each):

Set 1: 12 reps (rest 60–90 seconds)

Set 2: 12 reps (rest 60–90 seconds)

Set 3: 12 reps (rest 60–90 seconds)

Set 4: 12 reps (rest 60–90 seconds)

If the above 12 reps is successful, then: increase weight an additional 5 pounds (again: do four sets of 12 reps each).

Note: *If 12 reps are not doable,* do not *increase weight; just continue using the same weight.*

Time Off

Every 4 or 5 months, a weight trainer should be encouraged to take a week off to enjoy life and allow the body and mind to relax. After a week, your son's outlook will probably intensify the desire to train.

Put the Support Devices Away

These include wraps, straps, or any other support devices not recommended by a physician. I never had my nephew use them during his learning phase, and you should not introduce them to your son either.

A young lifter, or anyone who has been training with weights for less than 2 years, should never require a support device. If they do, too much weight is being used. Training during a learning phase should be used to strengthen muscle tendons, ligaments, and cartilage—and not to support them by using devices.

Even though I'm the leader in manufacturing customized weight belts and accessories, I do not recommend support devices for a young lifter.

When and How Training Should Begin

Your son's learning phase should commence some time before high school begins. First, he must always be accompanied by a trusted individual, whether it is his father, or uncle, or older brother, or just someone close who considers himself knowledgeable in the fine art of weight training.

Second, it's important to realize how easy it is to get started. Train in the basement; there's no need to run to the gym. Get him a bench, a bar bell, some free weights, a few dumbbells, and he'll be ready to go. You could save hundreds of dollars a year! Or, buy a couple of long-term memberships if you can do it on the cheap. Another reason he should not begin in an actual exercise facility is that you don't want to expose your child to the more advanced or elaborate exercise routines or equipment being used by trainers and other professionals who are training there. That will come later, after the learning phase. However, it may never come if he fails to possess the ability or coordination to experiment with basic implementations.

Conversely, if you really have your heart set on spending a few more bucks, then go ahead to the local gym with him by your side. By all means, go for it. Just remember to keep it safe and stay focused.

So What Happens Next?

Before he actually begins lifting, it's important he realizes that at this stage, a young weight trainer is learning form and acquiring muscle groove and should not be putting extensive pressure on joints and skeletal structure. This is not so much a muscle-building period as it is a form-perfecting period.

Right now, the emphasis should be on *number of reps,* rather than increasing weight. Weights should not be increased until he can perform 12 perfect repetitions.

Below is a list of the essential body parts to work on, as well as the basic exercises associated with each body part.

Muscle Groups and Exercises for the Basement Routine

Body Part	Exercise
Chest	Bench press
Back	Pull-ups
Shoulders	Side laterals (Barbell presses could have a negative impact on the back. He should not attempt any overhead presses until he reaches an advanced stage.)
Triceps	French press
Biceps	Barbell curls and pull-ups with palms facing in
Lower Back	Hyperextensions
Abs	Sit-ups and leg raises
Legs	Squats, ball squats, or free squats (Begin by using a broom stick. Never use heavy weight when learning this exercise.)
Calves	Jumping or calf raises on stairs holding weights, and one-legged calf raises on stairs
Traps	Shrugs
Forearms	Wrist curls

It's important to note there is a certain level of skepticism surrounding the idea of doing squats as a staple in his training routine. However, squats are the ultimate core workout. Some do not like the exercise based on the notion that an individual is susceptible to injury because of the design of the exercise. But I've never had a problem personally because I'm knowledgeable about the exercise. No one I've ever trained has had problems either. If you do teach your child this exercise, be sure that you know what you're doing as well. Having the knowledge is the key to preventing injuries, and we can't stress that enough.

After all, if you want to teach your son how to speak Italian, but you've never spoken a word of it yourself, it's going to be really tough for him to pick up the language.

The Don'ts

- Any barbell presses behind the neck or pull-downs behind the neck
- Chin-ups behind the neck
- Stiff-legged dead lifts
- Good Mornings—This is holding a barbell behind the neck, legs straight, and lean forward and come back up

Dead lifts are exercises that should be performed only at the advanced stages, and then only when accompanied by a professional.

The Workouts

Since the beginning, man had to physically exert himself every day one way or another. Cavemen had to hunt in order to survive. Hunting was a dangerous, yet strenuous activity that likely built muscle in the process, and they had to do it, dusk till dawn, and beyond, in some cases.

Even today, construction workers lift heavy objects daily and build muscle in the process. Baseball players swing a bat up to a few hundred times a day and build great big forearms and bat speed simultaneously.

It can be done, but we don't suggest it. For now, we focus on a workout regimen. The routine for the beginner consists of a 3-day regimen:

Monday, Wednesday, and Friday. Monday's and Friday's workouts will always mirror each other. (The beginner will go through the same routine.) But Wednesday's routine stands alone.

But in Week 2, the Wednesday workout from Week 1 will become Monday's and Friday's workout for Week 2. After 2 weeks, the beginner simply repeats the process.

If he should miss a day, or even two, always pick up where he left off; always keep the rotation going.

The following are examples of what 4 weeks of concurrent training will look like.

Workout 1

Week 1

Monday—Chest, shoulders, back

Wednesday—Arms, legs

Friday—Chest, shoulders, back

Week 2

Monday—Arms, legs

Wednesday—Chest, shoulders, back

Friday—Arms, legs

Week 3

Monday—Chest, shoulders, back

Wednesday—Arms, legs

Friday—Chest, shoulders, back

Week 4

Monday—Arms, legs

Wednesday—Chest, shoulders, back

Friday—Arms, legs

Workout 2

Monday—Chest, shoulders, triceps

Tuesday—Back, biceps, legs

Wednesday—Off

Thursday—Same as Monday

Friday—Same as Tuesday

Saturday and Sunday—Off

Note: *Each week is a repeat of the week before.*

Workout 3

Monday—Chest, shoulders, back

Tuesday—Arms, legs, abs

Wednesday—Off

Thursday—Same as Monday

Friday—Same as Tuesday

Saturday and Sunday—Off

Note: *Each week is a repeat of the week before.*

8 | Basic Workout Photos and Instructions

Steve and Doug

ABDOMINALS:

Leg raises: Using a chin-up bar, reach up and grab the bar with both hands. Lift your legs up, slightly bent. Lower slowly.

Position 1   **Position 2**

Sit ups: Lie flat on the floor, legs bent so knees are pointing up. Place your hands behind your head. Keeping your buttocks on the floor slowly raise your upper body up as far as you can and return back to the starting position.

Position 1

Position 2

Power abs (advanced stage):   Lay flat on the floor with your hands on the side of your head and your legs raised approximately 90 degrees and your elbows resting on your knees. Your spotter pulls on your knees and rolls you up so your feet are flat on the floor, and then rolls you back down. Keep your elbows on your knees at all times.

Position 1   **Position 2**

LEGS:

Squats: Using a squat rack, rest the bar across your shoulders. Feet slightly less than shoulder width apart. Slowly bend your knees and stop with your thighs parallel to the floor. Pause and then return to starting position.

Position 1   **Position 2**

Ball squats: Using an exercise ball or a basketball, start with the ball at your lower back leaning against a ball. Feet should be far enough away from the wall so when you squat you are at a 90 degree angle.

Position 1   **Position 2**

CHEST:

Barbell bench presses: Lie on your back on a bench, head and rear end flat on bench and feet flat on floor. Have the spotter hand you the bar. Lower the bar slowly mid chest and press back to starting position.

Position 1

Position 2

Position 1

Position 2

BACK:

Chin-ups: Using a chin-up bar, reach up and grab the bar with both hands. Pull yourself up and touch the bar with your chest. Lower back to starting position.

Position 1

Position 2

SHOULDERS:

Barbell shrugs: Hold a barbell with a shoulder-width grip. Arms locked, lift the bar trying to touch your shoulders to your ears. Pause and then lower to starting position.

Position 1   **Position 2**

Dumbbell lateral raises: Can be done either sitting or standing. Grab two dumbbells and with elbows slightly bent lift them to the side. As you lift, rotate the wrists so the little finger points up. Return to starting position.

Position 1

Position 2

TRICEPS:

French press: Lie on your back on a bench so the bar is above your head. Reach back and grab the bar and extend your arms. Keeping elbows in close lower the bar to your forehead. Extend the bar back to arm's length.

Position 1

Position 2

BICEPS:

Barbell curls: Grab the bar slightly wider than shoulder width and curl up until biceps are contracted, keeping elbows close to sides so not to use your lower back. Lower bar back to starting position.

Position 1   **Position 2**

Position 1   **Position 2**

CALVES:

Calf raises: Standing on a step or block, slightly raise one leg. Hold a weight in the same hand as the foot that is flat on the block. Rise up and down on your toes, stretching all the way down and flexing up on your toes.

Position 1   **Position 2**

LOWER BACK:

Hyperextensions: Lay flat on your stomach on a bench with your waist at the top of the bench and your upper body hanging over. Have a spotter hold your legs/feet tight to the bench. Go down to the floor and back up as far as you can.

Position 1   **Position 2**

FOREARMS:

Wrist curls: Sit on the bench with feet flat on the floor. Rest your forearm on your thighs or on the bench with your wrists at your knees. Roll the bar down your fingers and curl the bar back up.

Position 1   **Position 2**

If you have any ideas on new and innovative workout routines, submit them to www.howachampionismade.com for a chance to be featured in one of our upcoming books.

Evolution of

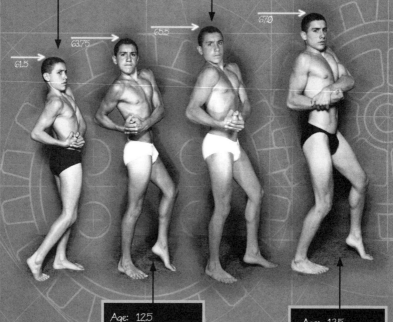

Age: 12
Height: 61.5 inches
Weight: 111 lbs.
Bicep (flexed):
R 10.75 inches
L 10.75 inches

Age: 13
Height: 65.5 inches
Weight: 126 lbs.
Bicep (flexed):
R 10.625 inches
L 10.625 inches

61.5

63.75

65.5

67.0

Age: 12.5
Height: 63.75 inches
Weight: 118 lbs.
Bicep (flexed):
R 11.25 inches
L 11.25 inches

Age: 13.5
Height: 67 inches
Weight: 143 lbs.
Bicep (flexed):
R 12.25 inches
L 12.25 inches

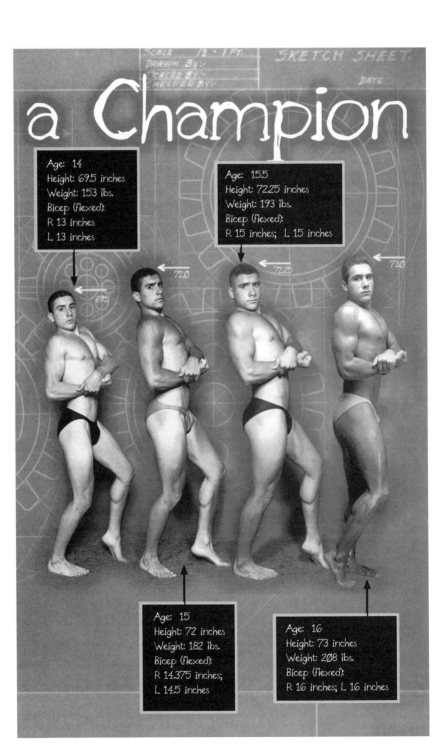

9 | Preseason/In-Season/ Regeneration Phase/ Off-Season

"Training as a young teen is extremely important for one's self-confidence and self-esteem. Kids nowadays pay too much mind to playing video games and less on finding the nearest pickup game with their friends.

"As far as the off-season goes, it's simple. The harder you work in the off-season, the more difficult it is to quit in the regular season. The off-season dictates the outcome of the in-season. Dedication to a good off-season program will compute to more tenacity when the score matters. If you don't commit in the off-season, you won't commit in the regular season."

—Joe Fleming
NFL Chicago Bears, Cleveland Browns
CFL BC Lions, Winnipeg Blue Bombers, Calgary Stampeders
NHL St. Louis Blues Draft Pick

Finding the right formula to ensure a consistent level of performance, on and off the field, 12 months out of the year, is something few people truly understand. The idea is to develop a regimen for your son in an effort to safely transition into his in-season—while maintaining the strength, endurance, and flexibility he worked so hard for in his preseason and off-seasons.

I had to get this right with my nephew. He may have lacked raw talent, but we looked to make up for it by gaining strength and maintaining it 12 months out of the year.

Below are examples of what my nephew did to stay competitive. It will work for your son, too.

Preseason

During this period, my nephew took the strength he gained in the off-season and applied agility and plyometrics.

Plyometrics is an exercise designed to develop quick and powerful movements, and can prove to be highly beneficial in competitive sports. Examples of plyometrics exercises involve stationary jumping, or bounding, which is a jogging motion focusing on pushing off with your feet and maintaining maximum hang time.

Your son can look to gain powerful and accelerated movements to improve his jumping, throwing, running, and hitting. The acquired strength from his off-season regimen should improve all facets of his game from a physical standpoint.

In-Season

As the preseason comes to a close, he'll want to back off the plyometrics and agility almost 100 percent, because he'll be doing a lot of that movement during practice. However, he should continue to lift with the goal of maintaining the strength he's gained in the off-season. To do this, he'll fall back to the same ideology used during his learning phase: less weight, more reps.

Knowing how much weight to take off the bar is essential if he is going to keep his strength.

It doesn't matter what the exercise is—he lowers the weight and ups the reps. This will ensure he maintains his strength in-season, and we already know he'll be flexible from the agility and plyometrics training he had before the season started.

He must train in-season—simply because kids are their weakest when they should be at their strongest at the end of their season, or postseason.

Regeneration Phase

The Regeneration Phase is a 2–4-week time frame that immediately precedes an athlete's regular season, or in-season, when his body is at rest. During this period, he should be walking, running, or involving himself in activities associated with any kind of sport.

Again, this phase begins when his regular season ends. At the end of his Regeneration Phase, his strength phase begins.

Off-Season

The goal during the off-season is to stay strong. Additionally, while weight training in the off-season, he must continue to practice or participate in his main sport while hitting the weights. If he hits the weights hard, he'll come into training camp, physically, a different person. His muscles will be bigger and stronger and will become familiar with any range of motion associated with his sport.

By practicing his art while lifting, he'll continue to maintain his flexibility and agility needed to play. The last thing he wants to do is hinder his physical abilities when they're needed most. So keep him running, jumping, throwing, catching, kicking, and swinging all year long! By doing this, the change in his body will be gradual and won't come as a shock.

But overall, this is a period in which your athlete is lifting his maximum weight and gaining strength. More weight and fewer reps are okay for this phase.

Keep in mind, this ideology applies to the intermediate or advanced weight trainer only. This philosophy should never be adopted by anyone training during their learning phase. No one participating in athletics should just weight train in the off-season.

10 | Train Barefoot

"When I started working out with them I could see a change in my lower body, meaning my ankles and calf muscles. And me, I run; that is what I do for a living; I run. So the five finger shoes, the Vibram shoes, were something that I thought that I could get an advantage over my opponent."

—Randy Moss–styleboston.tv
NFL Minnesota Vikings, New England Patriots, Oakland Raiders,
Tennessee Titans

My nephew was first introduced to training barefoot when he took up karate. In the gym, he'd wear flat discus shoes. It was the closest thing to being barefoot, and it added some protection if he dropped a weight on his toe. Both activities helped strengthen his arches. But he would ditch the shoes frequently. There was an underlying reason why he did this.

Peter was born with flat feet. It was severe. As a result, he was fitted for custom shoes designed to help support his arches. They weren't comfortable. So as a kid, he'd spend a lot of his leisurely and recreational time barefooted. Over the summers, at the family cottage, he would almost exclusively get around on his bare feet.

We began to notice a difference in his step. His calves had strengthened, and as a result, he became more flexible. When he reached the junior high level, Peter was already dunking a tennis ball on a 10-foot rim due to his extraordinary calf development. However, one month into basketball season, he began to regress. He was receiving support from wearing sneakers, rather than when he practiced barefoot. His muscles and tendons were getting weaker.

Recognizing this fact, whenever Peter was able to toss the clogs aside, he would. Whether he was playing hoop, training in the gym, tossing the football around, or performing his daily chores, he would lose the footwear.

But we weren't alone in our philosophy. Take a look at any muscle magazine from his era, or *Pumping Iron*, the 1977 film documentary directed by George Butler and Robert Fiore. In it, you'll see Arnold Schwarzenegger, considered by many, the greatest bodybuilder of all time, training in the gym barefoot. Arnold knew what he was doing. He saw the return on the meager investment of taking the shoes off.

These days, people are beginning to realize the benefits associated with training barefoot. Consequently, more and more professional and amateur athletic teams are reverting back to this philosophy. Barefoot training is natural, so athletes are now trying to catch up after all the years spent wearing high-priced sneakers made to give support to an athlete. In actuality, these shoes were holding them back. As a result, there is a huge push from major apparel companies to develop a product that can mimic the barefoot way.

The problem is, companies are taking a technology approach, rather than reverting back to a foot's basic elements. But after years of trial and error, the shoe that tops the list is the Vibram FiveFingers. The newly developed, innovative product acts like a second skin, providing the protection your feet need over a variety of terrains while allowing your foot to move like you're training barefoot.

I've been wearing the shoe for a year now. Over the course of that time, I've noticed a significant difference in the development of my calf muscles compared to all the years I spent training them in the gym, when I saw little to no progression.

Vibram FiveFingers is the way to go, in my opinion. Consider nothing else. Getting used to them may take some time, but there is no reason to get frustrated. And the great news is, the apparel giant is developing a shoe strictly for kids. Take your son to get a pair. Once he gets acclimated, then have him train in them. The results will be unquestionable.

Making a gradual transition to Vibram FiveFingers, I believe, will help your son build up the lower leg strength to begin training in them. Have him wear them for an hour just around the house; then 2 hours when it's comfortable; then 3 hours. Once your son feels comfortable spending a few hours at a time wearing the FiveFingers, he's ready to begin training.

I've found FiveFingers to be beneficial in both speed and agility training, such as plyometrics and weight training. For speed and agility training, they will allow your son's lower legs and feet to be more engaged and thus, more effectively build strength. During weight training, FiveFingers allow the wearer to stand on a level plane instead of with the lifted heel that sneakers force on the wearer. Being on this level plane better aligns the back and joints and will put your son in a better position to execute and get the greatest benefit from their power movements.

The FiveFingers aren't only for training. Your son can wear them doing most day-to-day activities, to the beach, throwing the ball around in the backyard, or going to the grocery store. Every movement in these shoes will be beneficial, building lower leg strength and improving his postural alignment.

As with any footwear, if he's wearing them in the gym or in the basement training with weights, make sure he's supervised. Though the shoe adds protection, dropping a weight with anything short of steel-toed boots on his feet could make for a painful visit to the doctor's office.

By wearing Vibram FiveFingers, your son will strengthen his calves, feet, and back—and decrease stress on his joints without even knowing it.

Hockey players rely a lot on their legs, especially their calves and ankles. If your son plays hockey, he's not skating 24 hours a day. When he's not on the ice, have him walk around barefoot.

But do the research. You'll find it's been proven scientifically that walking barefoot strengthens calves, knees, feet, and back. Additionally, it's endorsed by athletes all over the world.

Encourage your son to move about barefoot as early as possible in life. The rewards will be great. My nephew is proof of it!

11 | Bodybuilding

"In my 18 years of competitive experience, I have found that no matter how hard, heavy, or often I trained my chest, it would not grow like the rest of my body. Instead of spinning my wheels, I decided to embrace the body parts that did respond, like my legs. I am now known for having some of the very best legs in the division. This is not to say that I neglect my chest, but rather that I maximize my strengths and hide my weaknesses.

"Bodybuilding is all about illusion and by having legs that jump out and have a WOW factor, I have managed to catapult myself to the very top of my field. I did it the Cardillo Way! Thank you, Steve, for all of your help, knowledge, and insight. I am sure many others will be thanking you soon after reading this book."

—Jose Raymond
IFBB Pro

Bodybuilding is a comprehensive style to building an aesthetically muscular look. In most cases, bodybuilders look to compete against others, displaying their brawny physiques in front of a panel of judges keeping score.

Powerlifting, on the other hand, is more about strength than sculpting. It was the path I led my nephew down, and it proved to be beneficial: he was a three-time National Drug-Free Powerlifting Champion as a teenager.

There are three different types of bodybuilders, and each has their unique way of getting to the stage. I'll explore all three types in this chapter. I hope this aids those interested in getting the most out of a promising bodybuilding career.

Also keep in mind that the thought of bodybuilding or power-lifting should only enter the minds of those who are in their advanced stages of weight training.

Having the Perfect Symmetry

Symmetry is the most important asset a bodybuilder can muster. It's about having no distinct physical flaws or advantages but a perfect, symmetrical body that can be trained equally from head to toe. Consider the top three bodybuilding competitors in any given year of the Mr. Olympia competition.

If you reach the peak of the highest mountaintop in bodybuild-ing, you've made it to the stage of the Mr. Olympia competition.

It's tough to distinguish which competitor has the best overall physique on the big stage. They almost all look perfectly symmetrical, with no blemishes or major advantages over each other. How the judges come up with a proper score for these individuals has escaped me for many years. It seems as though their evaluation is random, and possibly for marketing purposes.

But these competitors have reached the pinnacle because they began their career with the most essential building block—symmetry.

Being Symmetrical with Few Flaws

The competitor's approach in duping the judges is to train those one or two body parts that lag behind more intensely than the rest. But that's not The Cardillo Way, so I'm not recommending it. This means that one has to double time it on the one that needs the most work, at the same time taking no time off from the rest of his body.

Examples of some flaws include:

- Narrow shoulders
- Flat chest
- Shallow abs
- High calves
- Small quads
- High biceps

A great example would be the late Paul Demayo, may he rest in peace. Paul, nicknamed "Quadzilla" for his freakish looking quadriceps, was a great success because of his uniqueness to one body part.

I trained with Paul. There were times Paul did not train his quads as hard as everything else because he didn't have to. He'd concentrate on his "weaker" body parts. But I can attest that Paul's "weaker" limbs weren't so weak. Because of this, he was able to compete on the big stage.

Keep in mind that one should never neglect a body part when training to become a professional bodybuilder. Put effort in all areas. The goal is always to be proportionate.

Demayo was amazing and a rare breed. Most of all, he was a wonderful human being.

I also witnessed Tom Platz train.

Tom Platz, nicknamed "The Golden Eagle," is a former professional bodybuilder who had one dissimilar body part from the rest, and that was his legs. They were obscenely oversized, but Platz was able to overcome his nonsymmetrical physique. Unlike Demayo, Platz took his best asset and emphasized building them up. His ideology was the complete opposite of Demayo, but it worked for him.

Platz was able to compete for decades, churning out a successful bodybuilding career, one that eventually landed him roles in feature films such as *8 Heads in a Duffle Bag, Book of Love,* and *Twins,* starring Arnold Schwarzenegger. He also worked closely as a consultant with Vince McMahon.

For the person training for more health and vanity purposes and not for competition, the Platz way is the way to go.

Arms Routine

As previously mentioned, my arms are my best attribute. Here is a workout which puts an emphasis on building up the arms designed only for someone in their later teens, once they've put the learning phase behind them.

Day 1—Triceps

Pushdowns 4 sets   10 reps

French press 4 sets   10 reps

Kick Backs 4 sets   10 reps

When warming up on the bench, be sure to put an emphasis on triceps, rather than the chest.

Bench Warm-up	*4 sets*	*10 reps*
Dumbbell Declines/Straight Inclines	*4 sets*	*10 reps*
Dumbbell Flyes/Cable Flyes (varies)	*4 sets*	*10 reps*

Total = 24 sets

Day 2—Biceps, Back, and Forearms

Biceps		
Straight Bicep Curls	*3 sets*	*10 reps*
Dumbbell Curls	*3 sets*	*10 reps*
Preacher Curls	*3 sets*	*10 reps*

Back

Pull Downs	*4 sets*	*10 reps*
Chin-ups	*4 sets,*	*until the point of failure*
Low Rows	*4 sets*	*10 reps*

Forearms

Wrist Curls	*4 sets*	*20–30 curls*

All reps are approximate.

12 | Steroids

"I was responsible for, and trained, over 400 professional athletes as a strength and conditioning coach. In my opinion, I believe the most common reason anyone would take steroids, or any other performance-enhancing drug, is to make up for lost time."

—Brian McNamee
Professional Strength and Conditioning Coach
Received Doctorate in Nutrition, an extensive study
in all fields of nutrition and health
International Sports and Science Association,
I.S.S.A. certified Fitness Therapist

Ain't Nothin' Like the Real Thing

This is what I preached to Peter, and it's what I hope you'll drill into the head of your young boy, too.

As a teenager, weight training and building muscle naturally far outweighs the benefits of using steroids to create muscle mass. The muscle that you build naturally as a youth stays with you forever. By the time an individual reaches adulthood, the body they worked so hard on as a teen is the body they'll have throughout their life.

Those who neglect to weight train as a youth but take steroids as an adult are making up for lost time and forcing the issue by accelerating the process of building big, lean muscle. The problem is that it's only temporary; it forces the person to continuously inject steroids into their system to maintain the buff look.

Additionally, building "real" muscle is healthy, both physically and mentally. It teaches a teenager to set goals, work hard, and achieve those same goals whether it is on the field, the classroom, or at work. Taking steroids is simply taking the easy way out. It teaches boys to be careless, thus making it more difficult to succeed in others areas of their lives.

By taking steroids, a person risks putting harmful chemicals in his system, and he increases his chances of being in trouble with the law. After all, steroids are illegal, and tampering with them will get him into big trouble, possibly banned from sports.

It cannot be stated enough: The main benefits of training as a youth is that a person will be able to see results early through his natural growth as a human being. Such results will fuel him to continue to work hard and eventually become great.

Moreover, a teenager's testosterone levels are peaked, so anything taken in excess could shut his system down and set him up for major problems down the road.

The Temptation

If there is one thing that *is* real about steroids, it's the temptation. We know a person will think twice before taking it, or not taking it, and while pondering, they may have to fight off the urge. It's only natural—no pun intended.

Parents need to understand that their children are under the same pressure they are under to succeed in this world. The temptations are real. If a parent was presented a pill that would propel them to the next level (giving them the opportunity to make more money, etc.), they just might take it.

The same temptation exists for the teenagers who strive to make the team, start at their position, or get to the next level of their sport; some just want to look prettier. "Do as I say, not as I do." (This is a parent's catchphrase indoctrinated by their parents before them, who may have made some mistakes in the past as well. It still works.)

The bottom line is: Teach your teenager to ignore the temptation.

But it's tough. The need to be attractive and buff is engrained in our brains. Society tells us if we want to look beautiful, we'll need to get big, toned, and be the proud owner of a six-pack. But that's no secret. That's been the message from the beginning of time.

Take a look at the statues of saints or ancient gods carved by man over the centuries—they all look as though they could grace the cover of any bodybuilding or fitness magazine today! Take Zeus, the king of the Greek gods and ruler of Olympus. In every picture or statue, Zeus is portrayed as an elder, maybe in his sixties, with white hair and a long white beard resembling Santa Claus from the neck up. But below the neck, Zeus has the body of a fitness model in his twenties, in the prime of his youth.

But if there is one way to combat the temptations your son may be experiencing, it's to keep the lines of communication open with him. Let him know that it's okay to approach you about the subject of steroids, or any topic.

Having great communication between you and your son may be the difference between him using steroids or not.

Has Anyone Died from Taking Steroids?

I've never personally heard of anyone dying from steroids alone. Conversely, taken in massive quantities, I believe it could be fatal. Taken in lesser amounts can, however, lead to other ailments that have the potential to knock you out with one punch. Steroids may result in high cholesterol and blood pressure, liver or heart damage, and certain kinds of cancer.

And these are changes that can occur immediately, or over a period of time. Either way, it's nothing your teenager wants to deal with. The same idea applies when it comes to developing severe acne. If your son is already prone to breaking out, steroids will make sure they come quicker than he wants, and with more potency. This is not a good look during his teen years! We know a lot of us had no chance; we were going to break out as a teen no matter what, but at least avoiding steroids can limit acne.

But there are other adverse effects as well, including depression, aggression, and even addiction, to name a few.

What Are You Addicted To?

It's important to note that no one gets a high from plunging a needle filled with steroids into their buttocks. I believe it's not a physical addiction but a mental one. Seeing himself grow muscle, gain strength, and look better at a rapid pace can be intoxicating. And this addiction, if not controlled, will only compel him to take more, increasing the chances of hurting his system.

But if your son can achieve the same feeling without the "juice," that is, if he eats right and knows what he's doing when he trains with weights, why not encourage him to do so?

There is a popular belief that steroids cause an individual to become hot-tempered, whereas normally, when they are off the "juice," they're cool as a cucumber. It's my belief that this is not the case.

Steroids increase the testosterone levels, so naturally, his aggression may spike a notch as well. But being transformed into a bully from a once kind, well-adjusted boy next door just shouldn't happen. Anyone who acts like a jerk on the "juice" was likely a jerk before the juice.

Doping Preseason, In-Season

Some athletes decide to take steroids preseason, or before they're ready to begin practicing with the team—maybe to give themselves an edge; perhaps to better their chances of making the team; or beat out the guys in front of them so they can finally start. Or maybe he thinks it's his time; the scouts are coming soon, and he wants to be at his best.

Well, what is he going to do at the end of the season when the playoffs begin and he needs to be at his best? It's obviously late in the season. By this time, he's lost some size and strength because he stopped taking steroids. Things might get difficult.

Another important factor to consider is, as good as he was on the field in the beginning of the season, off the field his emotional stability will also take a downward turn once he stops taking steroids. Something like this can most certainly result in the lack of production between the white lines.

So now what?

His addiction might take over, and he'll begin to dope during the season as well, getting himself caught in the vicious cycle of continuously cheating in the hopes his performance will continue to elevate on the field. After all, it's the postseason when he needs to be at his best.

By not taking steroids from the get-go and training properly and sustaining a sound diet, he'll maintain production on the field consistently, and will likely never hit rock-bottom emotionally. In fact, he'll feel great, enjoying all the benefits of working out naturally.

The lesson: The more he cheats, the harder his crash will be when he finally puts the needle down.

Other Side Effects

Will steroids cause one to lose his hair, even if his genetic code says he won't?

I'm betting against it. However, it may speed up the process. If someone is slated to begin losing hair at the age of 40, it may happen at 35 if he's injecting himself with steroids.

If what I said in this chapter was not enough to scare you, keep in mind that most of the steroids on the black market are fake. You will have no way of knowing where it came from or how it was manufactured. It could be motor oil for all you know!

Drugs, Tobacco, and Alcohol

Drugs, tobacco, and alcohol should never be used. This is no tolerance. Developing these habits at a young age will likely increase the risk of abusing them as an adult.

So once again, make a concerted effort to keep the lines of communication open between you and your son. Make yourself approachable when the subject of drugs, tobacco, and alcohol surfaces. Remember, you're not only his dad or guardian, you're his friend.

To Conclude

I'd like to wrap up by letting you know, and the rest of the readers out there, this chapter is meant to offer awareness of the negative affects of using steroids and to deter an individual from using, or even flirting with the idea of getting involved in steroid use. It's harmful to your system, it can render some serious negative long-term side effects, and it's illegal.

13 | How to Win

"I never knew a person that was bigger, stronger, and faster than the rest, but was not confident. It doesn't happen.
"Confident people are effective leaders in all aspects of life. The only way to gain confidence is to force yourself outside of your comfort zone. The more you experience, the more you grow as an individual. Through growth comes confidence. It all began for me by training with weights at an early age."

—Eric Kapitulik
United States Naval Academy, Lacrosse
1st Force Reconnaissance Company, U.S. Marine Corps
Iron Man Finisher
Mt. Everest Summit (April 2010)
Founder and CEO, The Program LLC
www.theprogramathletics.com

Winning. That's the ultimate goal, isn't it? To see your teenager raise the banner, trophy, or cut the net down and celebrate in front of your family, friends, foes, and everyone else in attendance. To see his team's moment of glory is what it's all about, right? He's a champion, that's who he is.

However, teenagers also need to know there's no shame in losing. If they leave nothing on the field and their team comes up short, they better respect themselves and their play, because anyone who witnessed the contest will do just that.

And young adults should always respect their opponent. If it's a player's opinion that the 20–0 thrashing his team gave out over nine innings was to a team of "terribles," then the victory was terrible, too.

In victory or defeat, he should always respect what he did on the field, and respect what his opponent did to try to stop him.

Giving Teenagers the Edge to Win

Does the fact that your son's opponents, the ones he unceremoniously swept out of the playoffs in round one, get to achieve similar praise for coming in any place but first tick you off?

I think it should. And I also think it sends the wrong message. That is, win and receive a trophy; lose and receive a trophy. What kind of motivation is that for your son and the rest of the studs in the league? Not much.

Have your son keep his own stats. It sounds individualistic, but at the same time, he'll be setting goals for himself. For example, if he knows he's batting .350 but wants to finish above .400, he'll focus more, dig in, and become ferocious in trying to get there. Home runs and RBIs are not excluded from the idea.

Today's teenagers are often being rewarded for their shortcomings on the field. As a result, we're stripping them of their desire to be the best, of their killing instinct, and of their will to win. We need to teach teenagers to achieve the goal of becoming a champion, a winner; and unless they reach the top of the mountain, there's no reason to make them feel like they did anything special.

Students don't receive A's just for showing up to class, do they? The Oscars make such a big deal of who gets nominated that it's difficult to remember who actually wins the Oscar. The hype over those who "almost made it" is a major disservice to the victors.

In sports, it becomes a major disservice to the youngster giving his all to reach the mountaintop of their sport.

14 | Top Ten Rules of Gym Etiquette

"I was barely a teenager, growing up in Texas, when I began hitting the weights. It proved dividends for me, because when I got to high school I hit the ground running.

"When football began, I never stopped. I carried out my work ethic right through to the end of the season. The reason was I never wanted the guy next to me to have an advantage. I'd run, do sit-ups, or flip tires if I had to, to get ahead. Furthermore, I knew by strength training early and often I'd have a better chance of avoiding injuries.

"Without question, training with weights as a young kid proved to be advantageous for me, all the way until my last game as a pro."

—Vernon Crawford
NFL New England Patriots

Believe it! Demonstrating the right gym etiquette can make you and your son's experience (and others around him) that much better. The following are the top "must-do's" when working out at any facility.

Before I took Peter to the gym, I made sure he understood what it was all about first.

Be Ready from the Get-Go

This doesn't mean remembering his gym bag, a change of clothes, or ensuring his shoelaces are tied when he enters the building. Simply put, this means: Make sure he puts deodorant on before he walks in the facility!

There is nothing worse, especially when someone is dialed in to a machine or particular exercise, when that smelly, bacteria-infested vapor cloud filled with another's oh-too-personal body odor approaches another person's workout space. It can be so bad it can break another person's concentration and can even affect his routine. Would your son want that done to him? Didn't think so.

Additionally, unsanitary conditions could lead to staff infections, an occurrence becoming too familiar in workout facilities these days.

So please tell him to prep, powder, or gel those cavelike, microbe-manufacturing plants called his armpits before he steps into the gym. It'll be greatly appreciated, I'm sure of it.

Respect the Staff

As soon as you walk in you'll have the opportunity to interact with gym staff. You may have to sign in with a pen or present your ID for scanning before entering the workout area. Whatever the case, be patient. Do not be rude.

There may be a line, a computer malfunction, or some other hollow reason why your entry might be delayed. Whatever it is, it will likely not be a big deal and will be corrected.

So, smile at the person in the front, abide by the rules from the get-go, and kick off a great experience for yourself, and make the staffer's life a little easier in the process.

Don't Be a Hog

It might be your favorite machine and for some reason, it delivers the best results for you. But it might be someone else's, too, or another member simply needs it to complete their workout. Either way, don't be a hog. Don't sit there all day.

In fact, at times you may see a sign letting everyone know there is a time limit on a particular machine. Most times it's for cardio equipment. Nonetheless, a sign is a rule, and you must obey the rules. If you don't, well, that's grounds for cancellation.

Respect the Professional

Respect that professional, the profound enthusiast who prides himself on finishing in a timely fashion. If your teenager is slow, or unsure of how to use a machine, he should let the person standing right next to him (the one waiting to use the piece of equipment and who clearly knows what he's doing) jump in with him. Your child is a novice; he should act like one.

If he's unsure of how something works and he goes ahead with the exercise anyway, his routines tend to be longer than the individuals who have a handle on working out. By taking a step back and observing a professional, he might learn something from them, not to mention reduce his risk of injuring himself.

So teach him to be patient and respectful of those who know what they're doing, and let them finish their business. Someday, someone will do it for him, too.

Do Not Scream or Grunt

Believe it or not, workout facilities are cracking down on the Neanderthal-like behavior that a lot of members are showing these days after a rigorous set. It's not cool, so give it a rest. We know you're there already. You don't have to draw more attention to yourself by whining out loud because you happen to overdo it on a set. Moreover, you're bothering the customers, and quite honestly, scaring some of them as well.

There may be a time when grunting is okay: If someone is working out in a power gym or in the weight room at school and he's surrounded by his football teammates cheering him on to get that last rep up, then it becomes okay. But he's not at that stage yet.

If he screams in pain, he's lifting too much weight; it has to stop.

Make Sure He Does Not Talk to Those Who Are in the Middle of a Set

Whether an individual is a professional weight trainer or not, they should never be interrupted while performing an exercise. It's rude, and it can be dangerous to the person he's annoying, or even to himself.

By interrupting someone in the middle of a set, you are causing that person to break his concentration. By doing this, anything can happen. The person training can drop a weight, lose his balance, or hesitate just enough to tweak a muscle the wrong way and end up in the emergency room—all because your teenager is a talker, or he couldn't wait to let someone know about what happened over the weekend at band camp.

Don't let him do it. He should be polite and allow people to finish.

Don't Let Him Walk in Front of Another Person at the Mirror

If a weight trainer or other gym member wants to work out in front of the mirror, that's his business; maybe he wants to ensure that he's performing a particular exercise safely and correctly.

Whatever the case may be, walking in front of him is no different than talking to him during a routine. It has the same effect. Doing that could halt a person's progress and/or cause a negative action to occur.

I doubt your son is a ninja or possesses skills to make him disappear. So don't think he's gone unnoticed, because he is. Tell him to stay out of an individual's lane during their workout.

He Should Wipe Down the Machines When He Finishes

A lot of people struggle with this one, but they should not need to.

There are few things worse on this planet than resting your head firmly against someone else's disgusting, soiled, greasy pool of sweat to begin an exercise. It's downright revolting, and it should not be happening. It's Germ Central, and you don't need any more of those, considering what's going around these days.

Teach your son to wipe that machine down as best he can. He will appreciate it when someone does it for him someday.

Make Sure He Puts the Weights and Dumbbells Back

A lot of new and innovative exercises are now being performed on DVDs or in the gym that do not include weights or dumbbells. However, that still does not deter the old-school weight trainer from throwing a few dumbbells around.

So remind your athlete to put the weights back. It's a courtesy to the gym that supplies them for him to ensure he gets everything out of the workout he wanted to like they promised when he signed up. Also, it's a courtesy to other members who can't find what they're looking for, or even worse, trip on one of them, causing an injury.

And we're pretty sure there are signs to his left, to his right, and even straight ahead drafted by the gym personnel themselves, letting everyone know it's not okay to leave weights or dumbbells, no matter how heavy, lying around the area—people can get hurt. At any moment his membership can be revoked. It's happened before. It's not just all talk.

Expect your son to be respectful and clean up after himself. After all, if he's strong enough to pick weights up, he's strong enough to put them back.

Wash Hands Before Exiting the Restroom

We can't stress this enough. The idea alone is vile. To bring someone's sweat and germs from his "holiest of areas" out to the workout area—it's unacceptable.

Not only is that person showing no respect for other members, including the staff, he's not showing any respect to himself. He's not a clean person if he gives the soap and water the cold shoulder on the way out of the restroom. In fact, he's not worthy of a membership.

He better respect the members and staff and respect himself by washing his hands thoroughly after using the toilet.

15 | Pat Downey, Life and Leadership

"At Gridiron Training, we teach the boys to overcome their fears by taking charge of a group and commanding a presence. We take them out of their comfort zone to overcome their fears. They will speak clearly with a good tone, maintain poise, body language, and, in turn, will earn the respect of their peers. At the same time, they're gaining confidence.

"They will fail, but that's how they grow, and so will your son if you get him uncomfortable to overcome his uncertainties about being a leader."

—Pat Downey
NFL Washington Redskins, Atlanta Falcons
AFL Nashville Kats
NFL Europe, Frankfurt Galaxy

Where my nephew became a champion in business, Pat Downey became a champion on the football field. I've known Pat for several years now. His story of how he rose to the top was compelling and inspiring. He was an underdog. He had to fight and claw his way to the top, and in the end, his dream came true. He'd become an NFL football player.

Because of his heart, discipline, determination, and leadership ability, Pat Downey became a champion on the gridiron. For that, I wanted to present his story to you in the hopes your son will better understand what it takes to become a great leader, and how to apply leadership skills to overcome adversity in life.

Pat Downey

What is leadership?

Leadership is the act of enlisting one or more individuals and giving them direction, inspiring or motivating to get the most out of a group, outfit, or team to achieve a common goal—to win.

A great leader will demonstrate sacrifice and will teach values such as accountability, communication, hard work, perseverance, loyalty, and integrity.

It's not a job or a label but a state of mind.

Anyone can be appointed a leader, but few can exhibit effective leadership; and few can express it like Pat Downey, a graduate of the University of New Hampshire and former NFL Offensive Lineman.

It was because of Pat's determination, passion, and resolve that he could lead himself and others effectively, and in the end, have his dream come true.

But as likely as Pat Downey is to swank about playing in the National Football League, he's more apt to confess he never thought it would happen to him; the teenager from the small town of Beverly on the North Shore of Massachusetts; the teenager who never meaningfully cradled his forearms around a football until the age of 16, or even had the desire to do so. Not a chance.

But that was him. That was Pat Downey . . . and it did happen.

Pat's first experience as a football player was for youth football when he joined the local team along with his neighborhood friends. After a short and sweet introduction to the game and after realizing his size made him a man among boys, Downey had second thoughts and decided football wasn't for him.

Though football would be a site seen in his rear view for a period of time, Pat's competitive spirit continued onward and he began playing baseball and soccer. Downey would continue kicking the ball around his freshman and sophomore years at Bishop Fenwick in Peabody, Massachusetts. It was there that the head football coach Jim Lyons took notice of Downey's talent and athletic ability and more or less told Pat with much conviction that he was going to be the starting quarterback for the varsity football team. Pat agreed and never looked back.

Downey's career began as a two-way player; suiting up as a quarter-back on the offensive side and cornerback and linebacker on the defensive side of the ball. In his first season, Pat was so hyped up being out there with the understanding it was okay to hit someone over and over and never be reprimanded for it that he played most of the season with two broken arms!

As Downey excelled on the gridiron, he would begin complementing his athletic abilities with a rigorous weight training program in the gym, lifting two times a day, every day, from the outset. And by his senior season, the scrawny teenager manning the posts on the soccer field was now one of the biggest, strongest, most formidable football players Bishop Fenwick had ever seen. Downey was MVP of his team and was elected to countless All-Star Teams.

As college loomed, Pat was considered a Proposition 48 athlete, which meant playing football for a division 1 or a 1AA program would have to wait. Pat's mom and dad decided to take on extra jobs to pay for Pat to attend Worcester Academy in Massachusetts.

Pat hit the ground running at the academy. He was named MVP of the team as an offensive lineman, a feat not easily imitated in football on any level. And the team itself went 9–1, tying the school's record for most wins in a season.

Downey had a tremendous football coach in Brendan Smith. He was a great leader and communicator and his technique was fundamentally sound like all coaches should be. He was a wonderful human being, and he genuinely cared about his players. Smith coached at a high level and demanded the same intensity from his players. It was that kind of effort and devotion that Downey had given; it did not go unnoticed.

Mike Stubljar, Downey's offensive lineman coach and English teacher, was one of the first to take notice. While attending class one day, Downey received an odd request from his coach and English teacher at the academy. Stubljar asked him to write his autograph on a white piece of paper. When asked why by Downey, Stubljar admitted he felt Pat was destined to play in the NFL and he wanted to be the first to obtain an autograph. When Downey played it off as a hoax,

Stubljar insisted. He wanted the inscription to read, *"To Coach Stubljar, thank you for everything, Pat Downey."*

Downey was stunned but obliged. And for the first time in his life, he started to believe.

After he left Worcester Academy in 1993, Downey verbally committed to Marshall University. He thought better of it and decided to play elsewhere for two reasons: He wanted to be closer to his mom, and sought to play right away.

He would receive a scholarship from the University of New Hampshire and play offensive line for the Wildcats, where he quickly made a name for himself.

Pat went in with a vengeance and would set the tone for every classman, letting them know there was a new sheriff in town.

As a test of strength, Downey was required to squat 235 pounds as many times as he could; and he was well aware of the record of 34 squats by a former player. Pat beat the record, and then shattered it when he completed 60 reps before he was asked to stop with more left in the tank.

Some were amazed by Downey. Some were threatened. Others just went about their business.

Pat led by example and became the team's leader on the field. Though he wasn't named captain at this point, his time would come. However, before the start of his sophomore campaign with the Wildcats, Downey would suffer a blow far more wicked than anything he'd ever faced on the football field. He was diagnosed with spinal stenosis, a condition which caused a narrowing of his spinal cord. He was at risk for paralysis, so he was told by his doctors, and he would never play again.

It wasn't enough to stop him. He shrugged off the warnings and set out on a mission to play football again. Pat would sit out the year and rehab. He worked hard, training and rehabbing to the point of exhaustion. Team trainers caught notice and thought he was nuts. He just wouldn't give up, and in the end, Downey defied the odds. He was cleared to play again. He was back on the field, and before he knew it, his senior year was upon him.

It wasn't customary for Coach Bowes to announce the captains for the upcoming season at the start of the final practice for spring football. That upcoming year was Pat's final one, and his last opportunity to put his stamp on college football.

He was nervous and tense when he jogged onto the practice field in anticipation of the announcement. But without hesitation, Coach Bowes named his captains, and the name Pat Downey rang out.

"It was the greatest accomplishment in my life," Downey has since said.

Coach Bowes told the group that Downey had received the most votes of any player who's ever worn the UNH colors under his watch.

It was Pat Downey's first such honor, and he'd take it to the next level. He sat the team down and went over the team's goals for the upcoming season. He'd convinced as many teammates as he could to stay on campus over the summer to work out and build team chemistry.

Downey spent countless hours putting together an off-season training program with the team's strength and conditioning coach. He also spent time setting up team functions, putting up signs with the team goals around the locker room, and sending out weekly letters to teammates reminding them of what they must do as a team to be successful.

Downey had been a leader his whole life, but it was his position in football that gave him the opportunity to influence and lead a group in a team atmosphere.

Suffice to say, after the team dropped its first two games of the season, something needed to change. With the #4 ranked William & Mary next on the schedule, Downey stepped up as the leader of the team.

Pat will be the first one to state it: Great leaders hold themselves accountable, first, and hold others responsible, as well. Great leaders put the team's well-being ahead of their own. Great leaders are great communicators.

Pat was just a young kid, and as a college senior, most have a difficult time finding the moral courage to take charge and hold their peers accountable for the better of the team; to put friendships aside and risk not being accepted. Not for Downey. In a mandatory team meeting, he took charge, held himself and the rest of the team accountable for bad play, and communicated effectively so the group could understand what needed to be done to turn things around. Moreover, Downey made sure everyone understood they were being held to a high standard; a bar set high as a result of a long, winning football tradition at UNH in division 1AA.

Pat empowered himself as a leader, and it paid off.

The team had a great week of practice, and carried the effort into the meeting against William & Mary. Any chance of lack of effort on the part of UNH would have been dismissed at the coin flip; UNH won decisively.

When the clock ran out that day, the realization of being the leader was a tremendous feeling. As the leader of the UNH Wildcats, it was a significant moment for Pat Downey.

UNH would come to play, and play hard, every game the rest of the year. When the season ended, they would become division champs.

After a heralded career at UNH, Downey was signed as an undrafted free agent by the San Diego Chargers. Pat remembers vividly getting cut in training camp, as well as the day Joe Bugel, then coach of the Chargers, let him know he could not play at the NFL level.

Once again, his dream of playing in the NFL would be in question. To get there, he would have to overcome adversity again. He was faced with a choice: to play on or go home.

Getting cut was a turning point in Downey's life. But the meeting with Bugel would fuel the fire that burned inside him.

After a 2-year stint in the Arena Football League, Downey returned to throw his hat in the NFL ring again. He signed with the hometown New England Patriots and was allocated to NFL Europe as a member of the Frankfurt Galaxy.

In Europe, Downey would play on a talented team led by former Heisman Trophy finalist, Quarterback Joe Hamilton from Georgia Tech. In the midst of his most important game, maybe in team history, Coach Doug Graber announced Downey as an honorary game captain. It was a great honor to lead his team onto the field on the day of the team's biggest game against the Rhein Fire, and in front of 55,000 opposing fans!

Downey would give every ounce of energy on every play and would continue to receive opportunities to play football.

Still property of the Patriots, Pat returned home from Europe and went to training camp for New England, where he would become one of the team's last cuts. Again, Pat's resolve would be put to the test.

A few weeks later, he would be picked up on waivers by the Falcons, playing most of the season on Atlanta's practice squad.

Before the season ended, Downey would once again change colors and land in our nation's capitol where he was signed and activated to the 53-man roster with the Washington Redskins.

It was a moment in the locker room, while glossing over the Redskins' program, that Downey realized where he was. And being there, out on the field before a game, was a defining moment for him. The Irish teenager from the small town on the North Shore of Massachusetts; the teenager who never played a game of football until he was 16 years old; the teenager who was told he'd never be able to play at the NFL level . . . had finally made it.

The following year, in 2003, Downey would be released due to a severe groin injury. In 2004, the Pittsburgh Steelers called for Pat. But after a team-issued physical, an X-ray showed a groin not fit to withstand a 16-game NFL schedule. Once again, Downey was let go.

The groin injury would ultimately lead to the end of his professional football career. But when all was said and done, Pat Downey made a dream come true by overcoming adversity. He did it by developing key life skills, leadership skills that would propel him to continually beat the odds. He was the underdog. He was told he would never play again. He did. He was cut a few times, got knocked down, and then got back up. Downey paid his dues.

In life, people face adversity. It's how they choose to face and conquer those harsh conditions that make them who they are. And when one becomes that great leader, they'll be a better person, a stronger person with confidence.

Through the years, Pat Downey developed and maintained scores of friendships, with many bringing great leadership and guidance. This pushed him to the next level as an athlete, as well as a human being. And no one brought more influence from a leadership standpoint than Eric Kapitulik.

"Kap" is a former United States Special Operations Marine and graduate of the United States Naval Academy. He founded The Program, LLC, an athletic leadership development company based in Quincy, Massachusetts.

Pat witnessed the transformation young student athletes were making; they were becoming great leaders under the tutelage of Eric. He was inspired, and a short time after being introduced to The Program, LLC, Pat made his move. He's now currently a lead instructor, working with student athletes at all levels on leadership development with the program. Because of his experiences in life, on and off the football field, Downey is able to instill these qualities in student athletes. The Program, LLC, has worked with organizations such as the Boston Bruins, NC State Football, and the University of Maryland Lacrosse team.

Pat is also the founder and owner of Gridiron Training, LLC, located in Boston, Massachusetts, where he enhances the athletic performance of football players at all levels, from youth leagues to the pros, through hardcore strength and conditioning training. Since his company's inception in May 2009, he's trained more than 400 youth, high school, and collegiate athletes, and now specializes in NFL combine training.

Today, Pat Downey is a loving husband and father, and a successful business owner. He continues to reside on the North Shore of Massachusetts.

16 | Peter Morel's Story: The Making of a Champion

"Peter was easy to teach. He was so eager to learn, and he strived to be the best in anything he focused on in life. Seeing him accomplish all that he has in life is the greatest honor I could have ever imagined.

"I'm proud of where he is in his life today—he's a true champion as a husband, a father, a nephew, and a businessman, and always will be."

—Steve Cardillo
President of Cardillo Weight Belts
www.cardillousa.com

Peter was an average kid: rambunctious, good-natured, and had an eye for teasing his younger sister like most older siblings do.

His favorite television show was *He-Man*. His favorite movie was *RoboCop*. And he could not seem to consume enough of those English Muffins topped with cream cheese.

Peter was born and raised in Everett, Massachusetts, a city known for its great sports traditions. But to say my nephew came from humble beginnings is an understatement. When he was just 6 years old, his dad passed away while his mom was pregnant with his sister. Less than a year later, his mother was diagnosed with multiple sclerosis. As his uncle and central male figure in his life, I took it upon myself to help raise him.

Taking Peter under my wing meant a lot of things. I'd be there for him in time of need, encourage him when he needed an extra push, and discipline him when he needed to understand right from wrong. And later, I would introduce him to weight training, exercise, and nutrition.

As a youth, I was fortunate enough to have an uncle teach me how to train properly. When my nephew Peter came of a certain age, I passed on my knowledge to him as well. I set things in motion by showing him body weight exercises. This meant push-ups, sit-ups, chin-ups, and many other exercises to get his feet wet.

From a physical standpoint, my nephew was an average kid. But when Peter reached the age of 12, I introduced him to more elaborate routines, which included working out with weights. Now more diverse, he incorporated an impeccable diet regimen from which he rarely drifted.

At the age of 9, he took his willingness, dedication, superiority, and skill, and entered the arena of martial arts by studying Kenpo Karate, a form of karate that emphasizes the use of quick, rapid strikes to overcome the opponent. At the age of 15, he was awarded his black belt.

He wasn't the most talented kid on his feet. However, he had a uniqueness about him. Because of his training in the gym, he now possessed the physical ability, the will, the desire, the heart, and the mental toughness to be competitive. These were components a lot of other kids did not have.

When he reached junior high school, he dominated his peers in anything and everything that involved athletics. The same 2 years he was the Presidential Physical Fitness Award winner and was captain of the team in eighth-grade. He was a member of an undefeated traveling basketball team and won numerous championships in the City Youth Program.

When he reached high school, he made the varsity basketball team as a freshman.

Through weight training, physically, he was now ahead of the curve compared to other kids in his age group, but the talent level of the teenagers was much higher now. So even though my nephew possessed the size and strength, the heart, the will, the desire, and the mental toughness, he was no longer as dominant as he used to be. He wasn't as talented as the rest of the bunch. However, he still played a major role on his teams, including his varsity basketball team that went to the state championship.

Peter was able to get to that level because of his dedication to weight training. It was the one thing that let him stand out from the rest.

Simultaneously, Peter was a three-time Drug-Free National Powerlifting Champion by the age of 16.

When time allowed, my nephew trained with Steve Collins in the ring. Collins, nicknamed The Celtic Warrior, was a former WBO World Middleweight and Super Middleweight champion boxer.

But Peter was truly inspired by a man named Joe Laurinaitis, better known as The Animal, from the professional wrestling tag team, The Road Warriors. Laurinaitis had everything Peter wanted. Physically, he was massive. He was athletic. He had character. My nephew would often try to emulate The Animal, and that was okay with me.

I kept my nephew busy at all times in the gym, dojo, or basketball courts to avoid hanging out in the streets and getting into trouble.

Peter was on a continuous path, challenging himself to succeed at everything he could get his hands on. He attended a football camp sponsored by the Boston College Eagles. While there, the Eagles coaching staff took notice and began inquiring about him. But academically, there was a wall standing in front of him I knew he couldn't climb. He was diagnosed with dyslexia. And in the summer before his senior year, he had to make everything up in the classroom, learning once again how to read.

The disability made things tough on him, but his will to succeed in life never wavered. He attended community college for a year after high school, but he realized it wasn't for him.

He took a job with Stop & Shop, one of the major supermarket chains in the U.S. I saw his strengths on the job. He was a people person, and it was his greatest asset. I wanted to harness his talent and watch him grow professionally. I approached him one day and suggested he start a business with me, operating a nutrition store. I thought it was a perfect match. He agreed.

I was fortunate enough to work with him—and he's been successful ever since. As a result of Peter's efforts, the nutrition store, American Nutrition Center in Everett, Massachusetts, is the most successful single standing sports nutrition and supplement store in the U.S.

He wasn't as talented as his peers, and he had to overcome a severe learning disability in life. But he got it done, so your son can, too.

It was an honor to witness Peter harness the drive, discipline, and desire to win and be competitive through weight training and athletics and become a true champion in life.

But keep in mind: Few people who train with weights are fortunate enough to have someone looking over their shoulder during every set who truly knows what they're doing, like Peter had. The less supervision one has, the more careful that person needs to be.

From the time he was 12 until he reached the age of 17, every 6 months I took photos of him, monitored the changes in his physical appearance, and recorded his measurements and the amount of progress he made training with weights. He was truly remarkable.

Peter dunking in Jr. High

Peter giving his sister a lift

Me and my nephew in Clearwater, FL.

Peter showing interest in training at age 5

Peter Me

Me teaching and coaching
Jr. High homeroom champion team

Peter 11 yrs old

Peter, senior year
in high school

Peter at 9 getting serious

Gridiron Training's Elite

Nick Bona—13 years old, from Peabody, Massachusetts. Star baseball player (3rd baseman) on the famous Peabody West Little League All-Star Team that went all the way to the Little League World Series Championship Game. Starting varsity football at Bishop Fenwick High School in Peabody, Massachusetts, as a freshman.

Austin Connolly—13 years old, from Salem, Massachusetts. Star youth athlete and black belt in martial arts in Salem. Currently playing football at Salem High School.

Ben Kaupp—14 years old, from Ipswich, Massachusetts. Star athlete in football and basketball. Currently playing varsity football as a freshman at Bishop Fenwick High School.

Eric Razney—13 years old, from Peabody, Massachusetts. Star baseball player for the Peabody Babe Ruth 13's All-Star Team. Currently plays high school football as a freshman.

Charlie Maistrellis—13 years old from Peabody, Massachusetts. Star baseball player for the Peabody American Little League All-Star Team.

Douglas James Garabedian

Height: 5 foot 9
Weight: 163 pounds
High School: Bishop Fenwick High School, Peabody, Massachusetts

Achievements:

- Varsity captain junior and upcoming senior year
- Became the first player in Bishop Fenwick history to record 100 goals for his career for the soccer team
- Leading scorer freshman, sophomore, and junior year
- All time leading scorer for Bishop Fenwick High School boys varsity soccer
- Catholic Central League MVP
- Massachusetts Olympic Development Program 4-year captain
- SF Vikings Soccer Club 5-year captain and 5-year leading scorer
- TopDrawersoccer.com 10th ranked player in New England
- National Honor Society Member
- 2010 Globe All Scholastic
- 4.2 GPA

References

MET-Rx
http://www.metrx.com/

VPX
http://www.vpxsports.com/

Gaspari Nutrition
http://www.gasparinutrition.com/

BCS Labs
http://www.bcslabs.com/

Here are just a few examples of some reputable supplement companies. Please note there is no affiliation between this book and any of the companies listed on our reference page. Their mention is solely based on my personal opinion.